THE LONG

The Long Way Home

GORDON BARLEY
with MIKE FEARON

KINGSWAY PUBLICATIONS
EASTBOURNE

Copyright © Mike Fearon and Gordon Barley 1996.

The right of Mike Fearon and Gordon Barley to be identified as authors of this work has been asserted by them in accordance with the Copyright, Designs and Patents Act 1988.

First published 1996.

All rights reserved.
No part of this publication may be reproduced or transmitted in any form or by any means, electronic or mechanical, including photocopy, recording, or any information storage and retrieval system, without permission in writing from the publisher.

ISBN 0 85476 454 2

Designed and produced by
Bookprint Creative Services
P.O. Box 827, BN21 3YJ, England for
KINGSWAY PUBLICATIONS LTD
Lottbridge Drove, Eastbourne, E. Sussex BN23 6NT.
Printed in Great Britain.

Contents

Prologue	7
Part One: Broken Dreams	13
1. Born and Bred	15
2. Various Positions	24
3. The Moon and the Son	32
4. Visions of Africa	48
Part Two: The Long Way Home	65
5. In the Mystic East	67
6. Beneath Burning Skies	83
7. Of Easy Virtue	98
8. The Edge of Insanity	112
Part Three: Getting a Life	125
9. A Window on Eternity	127
10. Living for the City	141
11. 'I Married a Monster from Outer Space'	158
12. A Sort of Homecoming	168
13. The Living and the Dead	180

Prologue

We were merrily swaggering down the roadside, the way drunks always do when they are pretending to be sober. Hushing each other one moment and laughing uproariously at our droll quips the next, my travelling companion and I were well sozzled. I was euphorically happy on my artificial high, without a care in the world.

Here I was, thousands of miles from home in the back streets of tropical Malindi, on the coast of Kenya, doing exactly what I would have done on a Saturday night back in my native London—having a good time, keeping an eye open for good-looking local 'talent', and getting a skinful. What a laugh!

'Now, whereabouts did we leave that hotel?'

Falling around trying to remember where we were staying, we were suddenly confronted by two burly African policemen. Each carried a powerful handgun, a lethal-looking baton, and had a large Alsatian in hand, straining on the leash.

We certainly weren't so drunk that we could be accused of being disorderly. We were just nicely 'merry', thank you very much.

Questions, questions. Why do policemen always ask so many questions? Yes, my name's Gordon Barley, for crying out loud! Look, here's my passport.

You wanna frisk me? What do you think I've got on me? Okay, okay, don't shove! Right, I've got my hands away from my side. This is like some cheap American TV cop show, you know.

Hands went down my side, fingers probing my pockets, and came out with a small packet.

I felt the blood drain from my face.

Look, I know what you're thinking, but it isn't like that. I can explain. That belongs to my mate, see. I was just looking after it for him.

The big African police officer sniffed the packet he'd taken from my pocket, then began to open it. For an instant our eyes locked: we both knew what it contained. My number was up.

Hands on me, pushing and pulling, scuffing my hair. I threw a desperate look to my companion, who stared stunned and disbelieving, as I was marched a few hundred yards down the road to the nearest police station.

The rich tropical air, which had been fried hot and humid by the pavements all through the scorching daylight hours, was now turning cold and dank. The vivid blue African skies were dark; the horizon spangled with bright constellations of stars I had never seen from my Romford home. I was beginning to sober up rapidly.

Hold on a minute, this isn't funny. Can we go back and do that differently, please? No, really, this is happening all wrong. I really meant to get rid of that stash ages ago, you see. Please, this should never have occurred like this. No, this isn't really me that this is happening to, is it?

Unfortunately, real life doesn't have a 'rewind' button on it. It's not like a computer game where you can 'save' a situation and go back to it later if you get wiped out a few moves on. There are no multiple options left on the menu when a heavily built policeman has your collar, and rough hands are dragging you none too gently towards a police cell. I panicked.

Call that a cell! Hey, I've seen bigger broom cupboards. That was a joke. Hey, why is no one laughing? No, seriously, this cell has already got people in it. 'Strewth, it's only about six feet square and there are two people in there already. It stinks to high heaven, you can't put me in here. No, stop . . .

How dare this be happening to me, I thought over and over. How could I find myself banged up in a filthy slammer, the victim of a narcotics bust, in the middle of Kenya? I was no criminal. Why didn't they listen? I wanted to tell them all about that stash they found on me.

There was only enough for a couple of smokes anyway—good cannabis though. I was only minding it for someone, see? Please come back and listen. Tell me, why do I feel so alone?

One of the travelling party with whom I was touring Africa had gone off on his own for several weeks and returned earlier that day with this gift—this small stash of dope, which I had carried around with me for several hours and never quite got around to smoking. I still had it in my pocket that evening when we went out to celebrate his return by getting blind drunk.

Come back! Let me out! This isn't a cell, there are no bunks, no furniture at all! There are other people in here, and the place sings like a monkey's cage!

Outside, a police officer began shouting. I heard crying, sadistic laughter, the sounds of violence. Looking around my new 'home' I could see by the dim light that the two lads, one African and one Asian, with whom I shared this minute prison were little more than children. The oldest, an Asian boy who looked about fourteen, was sobbing that he had made a mess of his life, and that his brother had set him up on a dope charge. The other boy was only about ten.

As I lay on the filthy floor, rank human odours besieging my nostrils, sleep evaded me. My mind was moving like an express train, throwing up memories of days recently past, the flotsam and jetsam of a life that had seemed idyllic until just a few hours ago.

What was this memory here, bright and vivid, like a surreal snapshot? Ah, yes, it was Nigeria, a few months earlier. The Sahara desert at dawn, with a flashing crest atop a towering sand dune: the first rays of the new day. The sky was beginning to lighten, curdling the night air and warming the frozen land. It was a memorable sight. The sun would send the temperature soaring up through forty degrees or more of centigrade within a few short hours. It was an unforgettable sensation to feel it beating on my back.

Like the perfect visual accompaniment to an epic Pink Floyd track, a clear and vivid azure sky had slowly unfurled, covering the trackless panorama of the black night, adorned with diamonds and hung with a brilliant crescent moon. Shadows accentuated the contours of the eerily shifting sand, stirred by the rising wind.

Now, as I lay in my tiny, overpopulated cell in Malindi, the sweat sticking my shirt to my back, I was rank with the smell of fear. The cold stone floor made me shiver, and the memories came pouring in again, pressed between the pages of my mind, haunting me like the ghost of Christmas past.

In Rwanda, we had gone off into the hills with two shotgun-toting tourist guides to protect us. We were heading for one of the few remaining forests—most had been cut down for timber, creating a massive ecological problem.

Suddenly, the guides had hushed us, and signalled for us to drop to the ground. There, in the middle distance was one of the rarest sights in the world—a family of gorillas in their native habitat. Like shadows in the mist a whole family of about a dozen noble creatures had ambled past us, arms swinging. At one point, I had been only a few feet from one of the young ones.

We had to remain crouched; to stand is to show offence, and to risk attack. The gorillas had stuffed great handfuls of vegetation into their enormous black faces, for these majestic primates are strictly vegetarian. Scrupulously clean, the father had easily been eight feet tall, nearly as broad and built like the proverbial concrete latrine. It had been a breath-taking sight, an encounter with a real-life King Kong.

Now, in my darkness, snapshot memories of wide open spaces—the burnished Sahara, the barren hills of Rwanda, and the African parklands of Tanzania—all made my minuscule cell seem smaller still.

The thought of those powerful, black gorillas, their fists like sledgehammers, reminded me of the vicious-looking guards who now held me captive. I prayed that they would prove as docile, but I feared the worst. I was trapped in a nightmare whose script seemed to be taken from the film *Midnight Express* . . .

These memories, playing like mental newsreels, gave me little comfort as I lay in my hovel. Eventually sleep came on me unawares, and overpowered me, carrying me off to sweeter dreams than my barren future seemed to hold.

In the middle of the night, I was woken by a hand on me. The youngest boy, scarcely into puberty, was making sexual advances to me. What background can he have been from that he thought this a normal approach to make to strangers, and what perversions had he known in his short life? I was shocked and sickened, and I rebuffed him.

We were kept awake by abusive yelling outside. At two-hour intervals, the guards marshalled all the prisoners out of the cells and hurled abuse at us. Whenever I was taken out to the toilet, I had to wade ankle deep through stinking urine. Paradise had turned into an ugly nightmare.

Oh God! Get me out of here!

PART ONE

Broken Dreams

1

Born and Bred

I am technically a cockney, born in Whitechapel Hospital, East London, on 10th July 1959. But most of my life has been spent on the edge of the Essex town of Romford—when I've not been 'globe-trotting'. I'm fond of that 'apples and pears' rhyming slang though, and I probably use it more than most cockneys.

My Maltese father was the black sheep of his family. When his parents emigrated to Australia, he didn't want to go, so he joined the merchant navy, got himself a few choice tattoos, and promptly jumped ship. My beautiful mother, whom he met in Tilbury, was painfully vulnerable to his sweet talk.

Apparently, the first time I saw my father was during visiting hours at Wormwood Scrubs; but I was too young to remember it. It could have been worse, I suppose; before he left, he could have named me 'Sue'!

All this information I gleaned later in life. I have no first-hand early memories of my natural parents, because I was adopted by a compassionate working-class family living out in Essex. My natural sister—two years older—had been put into a home before I was born, and three decades were to pass before we first set eyes on one another.

My new mum and dad were a soft-hearted couple who came from Stepney, but moved to Dagenham just after the war—then to Rush Green, on the edge of Romford, where they bought their own little house. For working-class people, that was quite a novelty then, before the 1979 Tory government turned it into a normal thing. Dad was a crankshaft inspector at Ford Motors, Dagenham. He had bad eyesight so he hadn't been allowed to join the army during the war.

Tom and Mary Barley were wonderful people. They brought me up as their own, though they made no secret of my adoption. They also adopted Sharon, very slender and pretty, a year younger than me but not a blood relative. We four made a loving family unit, in spite of the way we had been brought together by times and circumstances—each of us grateful beyond knowing for this shelter into which our broken dreams could be brought for mending.

Dolly and George, whose son I eventually came to 'knock around with' as a kid, remember my new mother first bringing me home, covered in rashes and sores. I'd obviously not been well cared for during my short life.

As a timid child, I loved drawing pictures, but I didn't really like junior school. Dark skinned due to my Maltese blood, I experienced bullying, rejection and racism from the other children, though I had some good friends whom I hung around with after school.

Daydreams of being a cowboy, or a soldier, a space captain or a footballer filled my young eggshell mind—anything but the reality of being a tormented little school child. I couldn't understand why I was so teased and outcast by most of the other children. I had become an outsider, a loner.

I always felt the odd one out within the extended family, too. Mum and Dad were 'mine' but these surrogate aunts and cousins never felt convincing, however hard they tried to be 'family'. The child in me was suffering from the loss of secondary relatives whom I could grow with and love, yet I never felt any great curiosity to know my real family and my real relatives.

My first holiday abroad came when I was eleven. It was wonderful, though I remember it causing some jealousy among some of the other kids at the secondary school. I started to make better mates there, friends I could trust.

Of the eight classes in my school year, I was always in one of the bottom ones, regarded as a real 'thicky'! There had been a system whereby if you came in the top three, you could be promoted to the form above. Then they changed the system, trapping people where they were, so I never could go up to a better class no matter how well I did—and eventually I started to perform very well indeed in some of my examinations.

The petty jealousy I had known early in my secondary school continued because my adoptive parents always bought me the best clothes. I was wearing Ben Shermans and leather brogues, while others in my class were wearing pale imitations of all this fashionable clobber! I don't think I was being deliberately ostentatious, but the 'have' and 'have-not' divide got up the noses of the bigger boys in the school.

Every weekend, the whole family went shopping, and my fair-haired sister and I never returned without a new present. I seemed to my envious classmates to be living off the fat of the land! I got a 'Chopper' mountain bike, but my best friend had to borrow my sister's bike whenever we went for a ride. You can imagine his embarrassment!

My young life nearly came to a sudden end one day when I was running around with my friends in the enormous fields at the back of our little cul-de-sac home, and caught my scrawny neck on a piece of barbed wire fencing. There was blood everywhere! I had come within a fraction of an inch of slitting my throat, or piercing my vocal cords. I was rushed off to hospital to be patched up, and to this day, I carry a jagged two-inch scar on my throat.

I was soon back at school. I couldn't wait to leave, and my classroom daydreams turned to thoughts of travelling. I became interested in geography, and it even crossed my mind to become a geologist, but I knew in my heart of hearts that I would never be able to get the academic qualifications. Physical activities—particularly judo and sailing—held a greater attraction for me than studying for stuffy examinations. Staring out of the classroom windows, I wished myself away to exotic and distant lands, sighing for a warm breeze in my face and foreign soil beneath my feet.

I was a member of the Boys' Brigade, and I vividly remember going forward at an evangelical crusade aged fourteen, drawn by the sheer emotion of the occasion, the extraordinary power of the message, and the fire-and-brimstone preaching.

There is no moment that sticks in my memory when I first came to the mystic realisation that Jesus was the way to God. I had always been taught to believe that truth from earliest Sunday school days, but I didn't know what it was supposed to mean to me in my own life. I had little affinity with Jesus, but I had a natural belief in God that stayed with me through my childhood and adolescence. Did God have his hand on me from that point? Perhaps. But my 'conversion' didn't last five minutes, and made no practical difference to my life.

Mrs Levick and her husband, who lived in a corner house three doors away from our little terraced home, were keen church-goers, recognised as pillars of the local community, and upright citizens. Several of us regularly went to her house of a Sunday afternoon, because we genuinely wanted to know about God. We wanted someone to explain to us, in a relevant way we could easily understand, just what difference it was supposed to make to our lives to believe in God, but nobody could! It all seemed a bit far-fetched, and I couldn't 'get my head around' the idea of living a Christian life. Though scarcely fifteen, my hormones were shooting around my body like meteorites, and I was becoming more interested in 'beer and birds', or in travelling the world as a rock 'n' roll star.

My parents never expressed any interest in religion, but I had started on a quest for 'spiritual truth' which no one seemed able to deliver to my satisfaction. But I remember vividly walking down the road with the Levicks' son, John, and saying to him, 'However much we stray from God, we always return to him in the end.' I little realised just how far the first part of that sentence would take me down the road to ruin.

I stayed 'religious' for a while. Boys' Brigade and attendance at a local Baptist church were part of my young life, though the commitment I made at that crusade turned out to be only a 'nine-day wonder'.

Clearing their enormous garden for Mrs Levick one day, I used Christ's name as a swear word.

'Don't blaspheme the name of the Lord!' she said sharply. I felt ashamed of myself, for she was such a sincere person it was impossible not to like and to respect her, and her rebuke has stayed with me ever since. The God who had been my childhood friend was more distant now, but perhaps it was me who moved away, not God.

I remember how proud I felt when I started in my first employment. I was still at school and it was only a Saturday job, but it certainly made me feel like a man. I worked in the butchers department at a branch of the Gateway supermarket chain (it was called Wallis's at that time). I remember my mother standing on the doorstep waving me off on the first day, so proud of her little boy.

My adoptive parents' twenty-fifth wedding anniversary was coming up, so I saved up all my earnings to buy Dad a cigarette lighter, and Mum a cameo brooch. She'd not been too well for a few months, so I wanted to give her something that would cheer her up. In the jeweller's shop, the jeweller said, 'You're very lucky. I wish I had a mum to buy all this for.'

Yeah, and I'll be buying her little presents for years to come. Won't it be great when I marry and have children? I'm sure she'll make a wonderful grandmother and—who knows?—a great-grandmother.

When the family went shopping, there were still those expensive presents, and there were always lavish gifts at Christmas. I was still spoiled something rotten, and it made a change for me to give a present instead of receiving one.

My mother had once fostered a child whom she eventually had to give back; it broke her heart. Having known the pain of such loss, she treasured me as only those who have experienced prolonged barrenness and had the gift of motherhood snatched from them can truly appreciate. And I idolised her in return. Now that I was working nothing would be too good for her.

In the mid 1970s, she became seriously ill although the diagnosis was only chronic asthma. She was never one to rest—she always had to be up and active, and even when she had to go into hospital, she rarely stayed in her bed. She would be up and about, helping out around the ward. The nurses thought the world of her.

She was receiving National Health treatment, but she was placed in one of the side rooms at the Old Church Hospital. I didn't realise at the time that those rooms are usually reserved for the seriously sick and the terminally ill. I was still just a child trying to be a man.

Mother had been a cigarette smoker, though she stopped when she became ill. I remember her racking coughs, and the shaking and crying out in pain. I made her laugh, performing silly impressions, but the laughter would soon give away to that deep hacking cough.

As she grew weaker, she was like a candle flickering in the wind, but still giving light for as long as she could. I screamed out to God to stop the pain and to ease her suffering—to heal her. Why didn't God answer? I couldn't begin to fathom such mysteries.

I was indoors when my aunt and uncle brought my father back from the hospital that last time. Sharon and I opened the front door, to see my dad coming up the path, distraught. As long as I live, I'll never forget the look on his face, like a frightened rabbit caught in the headlights of a juggernaut bearing down upon him.

'She's gone! She's gone,' was all he could say. My mother wouldn't be coming home again. *Ever.* Sharon and I stood there, stunned. For the second time in my life, I'd lost a woman whom I knew as my mother—lost someone on whom I had depended for the most basic necessities of life. Only a mother can love her son through thick and thin, always listening, caring, understanding, forgiving—always there when the chips are down.

A mother always sees the positive side of her son's mistakes and failures; is always there with a kindly word, a gentle cuddle, a hot meal and a warm bed. Always there. Though all the world deny me, I knew that my mother would always keep faith with me, a fountain of love that would always be there for me. Now she was gone. The sense of separation was devastating. *I felt a tremendous weight pressing down upon me, like six feet of earth.*

The death of a loved one is strange beyond belief. Perhaps I'd expected it to feel like the change from primary to secondary school, where certain classmates will be going to other schools, never to be seen again. But it's not like that at all. It's not like the ending of a friendship, it's more like losing an arm or a leg. I felt as though a vital part of me had ceased to function, and was gone for good. All my happiness turned to ashes, my cup of plenty into a bowl of emptiness. It was like staring into a black, bottomless pit. The days no longer had any meaning, and the nights seemed endless. Life went on around me, but I was playing solitaire.

There's no right way or wrong way of coping with death. My dad cried a lot, but strangely, I never shed a tear. My mother was worth much more than my puny tears; she was worth the sun and the moon, but nothing that I could give would bring her back.

Sharon coped by stepping into Mum's shoes, tearing around the house cooking and cleaning like a dervish. A year younger than me, she was only fourteen, and the burden was really too much for her. She had taken on a role far too big for her and she was crushed by it. She reverted to the absolute opposite of that enforced mother role and never really found her equilibrium again.

The post-mortem showed that Mum had not been suffering from asthma, but from lung cancer. She was only forty-six, but when we saw her laid out in the Chapel of Rest, she looked eighty! All I saw was an aged corpse, an inadequate relic of my mum. I recoiled in shock, hardly believing that this burnt-out shell was really the woman I knew as my gentle and kindly mother. Sharon sobbed her eyes out, but I still couldn't, and I felt guilty for not crying.

Father David took the funeral service, bringing a sense of peace and dignity to the occasion.

Dad, Sharon and I were in a daze for months afterwards.

I carried my pain about with me like a sacred relic, desperately holding on to it as though it were the only thing that still connected me with my mother. I felt as though my life was severed in two; I was trapped in the present while my mum was the other side of a heavy curtain in the past. *She was now in a room that I couldn't enter this side of my own death.*

I knew that I had to be strong. Sharon and Dad needed me, and I could no longer afford the luxury of grief—I had to be the one who held us all together. Later, Sharon sometimes coped by swearing and using foul language, which my father hated. I tried to keep the peace between them, though I was barely sixteen years of age.

In the dark days that followed, I felt terrible guilt for going to a dance so soon afterwards. I spoke to an old school friend there, whom I knew had lost his own mother at an early age, and found some comfort; but emotionally, I was in a turmoil. I kept opening my mouth and putting my foot in it, with inappropriate remarks. I didn't feel 'in my right mind', and everything I said and did seemed wrong.

As anyone who has known the pain of bereavement will know, you don't wake up one morning and think, 'That's it! My grief is over and done with. Time to get on with living!' For most people, the aftermath drags on—sometimes for years.

Dad had been working shifts at Ford Motors, but reverted to permanent day shift in order to spend more time with Sharon and myself. Me? I learned to hide my pain, and to pretend that I was a tower of strength, when really I was a lost little boy who desperately wanted his mum.

The deceit had begun.

2

Various Positions

In 1975, I left school—with almost no qualifications. I was sixteen, and had precious little confidence in myself.

I was fond of art and toyed with the idea of going to art college, but the desire to make money came first. I wanted a secure, well-paid job, and I remember being knocked back when I was rejected for a job at Ford Motors, though truthfully I was never really cut out for factory work.

When applying for jobs, I exaggerated my paper qualifications on all the application forms, hoping that these wouldn't be followed up. This scam didn't work for long. With the light bulb company that first employed me, I constantly loused up the calculations they had given me to do on the strength of my gleaming mathematics 'qualification'. It didn't take long for the light to dawn on my employer that my paper qualifications were as legitimate as a £6 note, and I was soon 'out on my ear'. But within a few hours I had found myself a better job as a messenger clerk with a leading shipping company in Holborn—a position that would enable me to get out and about, visiting embassies and consulates for documents to be processed.

Though everyone else in the office spoke in excited tones

of their hopes of advancement and promotion, and the extra money would certainly have come in handy, the job was a very long way from those pictures of far-away places I'd seen on the walls of the high commissions and embassies which I frequented. The thought of visiting them made my mouth water.

So after a year I found another job with better prospects and more money, in a larger company. Starting as a postal clerk, I quickly climbed to the dizzy heights of the accounts department. Checking audits was a simple enough job, but I soon became bored out of my skull. Work was one long yawn, and I yearned for a bit of adventure.

I began going out to trendy pubs, clubs and discos, and doing all the things that healthy young men usually do. As I became more outgoing and sociable, my self-esteem slowly began to improve. I was still involved with a youth group at Main Road Baptist church and although I didn't go to church every Sunday, it was still an important part of my life. An emotional longing was struggling within me, not simply a mounting sexuality, but a lust for what I could only describe as 'inner union', of a type that didn't totally conform to my Baptist background.

Once, in a prayer meeting, I prayed for 'peace on earth and a uniting of all religions'. An elderly man promptly stood up and proclaimed, 'In the name of Jesus, there is only one God, only one Lord, and only one way to eternal salvation!' He wasn't having any truck with wishy-washy liberals like me. Yet, afterwards, a girl came up to me and said that she had found my prayer very beautiful. Liberal ideas are often far more attractive than uncompromising truth and, for the moment, anything and anyone I found attractive was certainly going to get my vote.

My churchgoing caused some 'ribbing' from my mates in the pub afterwards. One mate, Trevor Bacon, was a strong influence on me. He was heavily into Confucianism, Buddhism, mysticism, macrobiotics and other New Age ideas. We would talk till the early hours about 'the human condition', fortified by a supply of drink and drugs. Trevor's ideas about Eastern philosophy quickly rubbed off on me. I was attracted to the popular New Age philosophy which sees the individual as more important than a relationship with God on his terms.

When an early girlfriend invited me to her school disco, she was apologetic that I wouldn't know anyone there. Yet the moment I walked through the school doors, another girl exclaimed loudly, 'I don't believe it's him! He's here!' A little group of her friends became very excited, too. I recognised her as a member of a climbing club to which I belonged; she had been on some trips we had made to the Lake District.

Still burdened with a low self-confidence, it was only dawning on me slowly that women could find me sexually attractive. It took my breath away, and set my girlfriend back a bit—particularly when I bumped into another group of girls I knew from the church youth group, who all began competing for my attention. I remember my steady girlfriend coming back from the toilets with tears in her eyes because of the 'superstar' reception I had received! My shaky self-image began to soar, as I realised that I wasn't as unattractive as I had thought. *'Hey, I'm really quite a guy, aren't I?'* I began to believe.

My sister suffered from my increasing self-absorption to nearly the same extent as my long-suffering girlfriend. On a family holiday in Bournemouth, Sharon tagged along when my mate Dave and I picked up a couple of girls for a walk along the sea front. I wasn't having my sister cramping my style so I sent her away. I later felt guilty about being so callous.

Returning to Romford from work each evening, I began to get to know some of the other commuters around my own age who made the same journey at the same time each day. An 'older woman' among that group (I think she was all of twenty-one while I was eighteen!) began to meet me platonically for long discussions. Lisa explained that she had been forced to split up with a boyfriend because she was Jewish and her parents didn't approve of her dating a Gentile gentleman.

Lisa and I would often talk late into the evening, until one day the inevitable happened—in the wee small hours, she seduced me. I lost my virginity to her in confusing and unsatisfactory circumstances. She didn't want a proper emotional relationship with me—I was just someone to have around as a comfort blanket. I don't believe that she ever really desired me; she merely needed to *be* desired and loved. My initial shock changed to fear fused with excitement at these new pleasures.

The next night I was supposed to be taking my regular girlfriend—with whom I had never slept—off to a party. In preparation for the evening's festivities my mates and I had been to the hairdresser, like a bunch of pansies, and on the bus back I chatted up two attractive girls—inviting them to the party though not expecting them to come. Not content with dangling two girls on a string, I wanted two more!

It was likely to be a typical lads' party with few girls present, so I rationalised my actions by saying to myself that I was collecting them 'for my mates'. At the party, I was standing next to my long-suffering girlfriend when one of the two new girls showed up, and refused to talk or dance with anyone else but me. She was indignant that I had invited her to a party and then turned up with another girl. Not surprisingly, both of them soon concluded that I was a walking disaster area as far as any long-term relationship was concerned. I packed in my regular girlfriend, and I was soon left with just my older lover—for a time, anyway.

Lisa explained that people had been constantly asking

her what was wrong with her, because they thought she looked so unattractive. Yet I found her to be a lovely, bubbly energetic person—albeit a bit of a hypochondriac. She might have made a typical Jewish mother, had she not died suddenly of a stomach problem. I remember the funeral service: no flowers, just a bare coffin, and a feeling of great emptiness. The nights of laughter and soft lies had ended. It felt for a moment like my mother's death all over again and I felt desolate.

Soon there was a new woman in my life—I seemed to change them as often as I changed my socks. Gail was a beautiful girl, but I treated her badly for the year that we were together, because she wanted to marry me and I wasn't truly interested in a permanent relationship. Two bereavements in such a short time made me frightened to give my love wholeheartedly to a new woman in case I lost her suddenly and irrevocably. I kept poor Gail hanging on, like an ornament on my arm—and in my bed.

Looking back, it's curious how I became so promiscuous. As a child, I had entertained romantic notions of marrying in a fairytale wedding, and living happily ever after. That view of lifelong love didn't last for very long. Page three pin-ups and the gossip of my friends spurred me on to new heights of licentiousness.

All my girlfriends were interested in long-term relationships, with only an occasional girl who was satisfied with a one night stand. From being seduced, I had become the seducer—though I never forced anyone into my bed. It takes two to tango.

My sister had a wild time herself, but it's different for girls; their biology has a habit of catching up with them. She had a job for six months, but got the sack because of all the two-hour lunch breaks she took to spend time with her boyfriend and lover, John. She was out of work and pregnant at the age of seventeen. He was a lanky brown-haired

West Ham fan, with whom I got on very well. We both loved old rock'n'roll music.

They married, for better or for worse; and it proved to be the latter. John was confused and upset by Sharon's inability to cope, which probably stemmed from the trauma of losing her mother at a critical age. They lived in a council flat on the Marks Gate estate, and more often than he can remember John came home from his job to find the place a complete tip, with strange moulds growing behind the refrigerator, and the sink piled high with filthy dishes. It was no fit place for the baby, Clare, at whom Sharon shouted loudly and often. My little sister just couldn't cope with the twin pressures of marriage and motherhood. Her condition was put down to post-natal depression but it showed little sign of lifting.

In 1978 she spent several months in hospital, seldom visited by John, who was finding it very hard to cope with her condition. Most of us live on the edge of a mental and emotional precipice, so it is not surprising that some occasionally fall over the edge.

I could certainly relate to the grey spectre of depression which Sharon had encountered, but that deep dark night of the soul was outside of my experience. I lived in fear of following her, and going far beyond into the wild and demented realms of insanity. I dreaded the coming of crazed visions that would tip me into delirious raving and derangement.

John had stood by Sharon as best he could, trying his hardest to be a good husband and to make the marriage a success. I couldn't blame him when he decided to cut his losses and apply for a divorce. Like him, I resented the emotional manipulation, and I was guilty of trying to brush her condition under the carpet or to wish her away. John and myself remained good friends after the *decree nisi*, and my niece was brought up by John's parents.

I could have been married myself to any one of many lovely women, but I blew them all out, both because of the echoes of my lack of confidence and through a reluctance to settle down too young. I wanted to keep tasting the fruits of this world.

I believe that my success as a Romeo owed much to my listening ear. I was always a good counsellor and confidant, which once led me to join the Samaritans, where this gift might have been put to wider use. I had two interviews and was soon accepted onto a training course. During the course, I realised that I wasn't ready for the long-term commitment that was required to become a Samaritan. My head was still full of thoughts of global travel.

Hill walking and rock climbing had been my favourite pursuits since my mid-teens, and I was a keen member of the local climbing and mountaineering club. When Ray, whom I met through the Levick's and the local Baptist church, invited me to go scrambling with him in Austria, I jumped at the opportunity to get abroad. I imagined that I was in for a fabulous time: I couldn't have been more wrong. After a preliminary trip to Scotland—a freezing tent in the Cairngorms in November is not my idea of fun—we were off on an even more disastrous trip to the Alps. We certainly rubbed each other up the wrong way—I went for him with an ice axe at one point! Somehow, we managed to tolerate each other and get home in one piece. The stunning scenery was better than the company . . . At one point we nearly fell through the ice layer into a freezing lake, so all in all I think I am lucky to be still alive. Ray seemed oblivious to the poor quality of my meagre equipment. It's a bad idea to go out onto the mountains without the proper gear, but my companion seemed more concerned about having someone to go with him than about his partner's comfort and safety.

Up in the peaceful mountains, I made a promise to

myself that I would do my best to live harmoniously with my family, and to get back into harmony with God. But it was a naive and false promise.

When I returned, I continued to hurt my father by being distant from him. My sister was his blue-eyed girl, while I had been the light of my mother's eyes. We had the best of everything, we never had to do any work around the house, we were waited on hand and foot, but I repaid my father's love and care with thoughtless and hurtful words. I lost my rag with him at one party when, to my disgust, he put on a Max Bygraves record, and an uncle took me aside to rebuke me for my lack of respect and poor manners.

It was around this time that I bumped into Gary. He was a northerner who was selling a leaflet called *One World*, asking for money for 'missionary work'.

'What sort of missionary work?' I asked him.

'Oh, all sorts of charity projects overseas.'

I was impressed by the way Gary was clearly doing something in which he believed, standing out on his own regardless of ridicule or the cold December weather. Nothing was going to deter him from telling others about his faith.

Gary invited me to attend a weekend of seminars to find out more. I told him that I would think about it. The following weekend I flew off for two weeks' holiday in Switzerland. During that time, I said to my holiday companion that I was thinking about becoming a 'born-again Christian'.

'Don't be so stupid!' was my friend's gruff reply.

When I returned to Britain, Gary was surprised to hear from me again, but he was pleased to arrange for me to spend a weekend with the Unification Church.

I was on my way to becoming a 'Moonie'.

3

The Moon and the Son

January 1979 found me on a weekend course at Lancaster Gate, West London, courtesy of the Unification Church. We slept comfortably in bunk beds in modest rooms, but the communal rooms—the lounges, kitchens and lecture halls—were all lavishly equipped. It was like being in a five star hotel or a plush millionaire's home.

But more overpowering than the palatial surroundings were the intensity and depth of the relationships which blossomed over the weekend. It's called 'love bombing'—making someone feel valued as a person in their own right by bestowing on them the dignity which the rigours of everyday life have stripped away. Hugging and frequent enquiries about one's welfare are the common features of this approach. There's nothing wrong with that in itself, of course, unless it is done for a sinister purpose.

At Lancaster Gate I enjoyed meeting interesting people from all over the world, many of them young students. All of us were very vulnerable and impressionable. The morning began with a brisk walk around Hyde Park, returning for the first of several two-hour lectures. The first talk was concerned with the various periods of history—a potted version of cult leader Sun Myung Moon's book *Divine*

Principle. I was very attracted by the eastern philosophies which peppered the talks, laced with a wacky form of Christianity to which I quickly warmed.

After this weekend I was invited to stay on for an intensive seven-day workshop to find out more about this strange and wonderful religion which seemed to offer so much. It was an exciting place to be, with the bait held before me of many more secrets which would be divulged to me should I wish to partake of the week-long course.

I took the bait, hook, line and sinker. I felt alive, surrounded by caring and vibrant people. Years later I discovered that this 'love bombing'—the initial enthusiastic smothering of potential members with encouragement—is a classic cult recruitment technique.

I slept badly on the first night of the seven-day workshop, and the trip out to Hyde Park for some physical exercise without so much as a cup of tea inside me got me off to a bad start. We all had chores to do after breakfast, then the first lecture proved to be very basic, so I didn't feel the same enthusiasm that I had felt on the two-day course; but I gradually began to perk up.

The second day was much like the first, except for a game of 'rounders' in the afternoon. It was enjoyable, though I was bemused and bewildered by it all. I found that the two-day course had been very necessary before the seven-day marathon, because without the preparatory talks behind me, I would have been very confused.

In the group sessions we began to talk about our personal problems and to get down to the nitty gritty, so to speak, instead of skimming the surface. I wrote at the time: 'We are beginning to feel that we can be really open, and to talk about what is really bad in us, in turn being honest with ourselves, accepting the sinful way we have lived in the past, looking to God for spiritual guidance, and doing something positive to change.'

By the third day I felt spiritually elevated and was able to understand the challenging lectures more clearly. I tried to break the ice with the group by speaking candidly about my own sexual problems. Reading back through my diary, I realise that I was completely hooked by the teachings of the Unification Church, seeing them—perhaps wrongly—as an expression of my own spirituality.

Day four brought us to exciting teaching about the second coming of Christ. I was fascinated and enthralled to hear that the Saviour was living on this earth. But who was he, and where was he? Could it be this Korean prophet called Sun Myung Moon they kept talking about? No one said it was so at this stage but they implied it. I felt indescribable joy! It's extraordinary how easily you can make yourself believe untruths simply by desperately wishing for them to be true, and using wish fulfilment to create your own reality.

The *Divine Principle* had completely indoctrinated me, and my new-found friends warned me not to slip back into my old ways of living. They suggested that I should burn all my old clothes, because they were tainted with an unworthy and sinful lifestyle. I drew the line there, though I suffered the inevitable pangs of guilt afterwards in the face of the elders' condemnation. I was also encouraged to abandon my old family and friends in living my new life for Jesus—as revealed in Sun Myung Moon's awesome teachings—but I wasn't going to do so.

Yet I was delighted to know that I had a spiritual father in Mr Moon, who could lead me through to my salvation, calm the storms raging within me, and help me to overcome my sexual appetite. I wrote in my diary: 'The more I talk about this problem, the more I am sure spiritually that when the lustful spirits come to me I will have the power and the faith to fight them off.' I was told by another group member: 'Many with the same problems are waiting for your understanding, prayer and help.'

Writing, drawing and creating took up the afternoon of the fifth day. This burst of creativity opened up most of our group to understand their own problems, and to talk honestly about their situations. Alphonso and Gabrielle were two in the group who were moving spiritually in the same direction as myself. Alphonso often intellectualised his spiritual life, and asked technical questions about the *Divine Principle*, instead of simply opening up himself to God's love.

During the seven-day course, we all trooped off to see the film *Superman*, which had recently been released. On the way back, we spoke about 'spirit men' and how Superman was the embodiment of a good 'spirit man'—in the sense of a ghost waiting to enter the body of a living person with similar spiritual beliefs. Few people realise that much of the underlying theology of the Unification Church is spiritist. I blithely said, 'It's pointless worrying about the spirits because they will lead us this way and that. We need to concentrate wholeheartedly on God.' I was quite indignant about this strange attitude towards the spirit world which, even at that time, I began to think was a little bit suspicious; it didn't seem 'right', though I was unaware then that it was profoundly unbiblical.

These people treated the Bible as God's word, but considered that the fullness of God's revelation was found only in the *Divine Principle*. Consequently, we were never encouraged to read the Bible—nor was it central to the Unification Church's teachings.

According to their teaching, before Adam had sex with Eve, she was seduced by Lucifer, appearing as a man. Cain, the offspring of this union, began the lineage leading up to communism. Abel, Adam's child, started the line leading up to spiritual democracies in Korea and the United

States—or so I was told. Because God's original purpose of breeding a perfect family through Adam and Eve had been thwarted, Jesus Christ had to come to marry, and to raise a perfect family; but before he could find his Eve and procreate, he was killed. 'The Cross is the symbol of Christ's failure,' according to Sun Myung Moon—though you certainly won't find *that* idea in the Bible.

As the week's course drew towards its conclusion, I knew that I was looking for a deep and loving relationship with God. The Unification Church leaders suggested that, instead of going back home, it would be better for me to spend some time in their country residence, to give me space to let that relationship develop. Mark, our leader, told me that I would be able to learn how to help others to take the step that I had taken. I agreed to go out to the country for twenty-one days. My father and my current girlfriend, Gail, both seemed upset when I told them about my decision over the telephone.

Dad was saddened by my interest in the Unification Church. I'm sure he would rather I married like my sister, and had 2.4 kids, but that kind of commitment frightened me. But he was resigned: 'If that's what you want, son, then I'm happy for you,' he said. He understood my heart for adventure, and the sense of excitement I felt about the unknown.

The course was held at Livingstone House, a former convent that had been bought and given to the Unification Church by devotees as a training centre and retreat house. Looking back, it was not so much a peaceful place to recuperate and get back into the world, as somewhere to run away to escape the world and all its problems.

Livingstone House was gigantic. We explored room after room, and spent time cleaning while the girls cooked a meal for the twelve of us on the twenty-one-day workshop in the bright winter countryside. 'I think we will get on all right,' I wrote. The food was wholesome and good. There was no sleep deprivation—a common tactic with many subversive cults—though some of the talks seemed to stretch till late into the night.

We were given many inspirational lectures on this third course, though I found them difficult to understand. No one said outright that Sun Myung Moon was the Messiah, though this conclusion was strongly hinted. I would learn more as I stayed at this beautiful country house, I was told.

Because Christ's mission was a dismal failure, God had to find another set of parents to live a sinless life dedicated entirely to God, and to succeed where Adam and Christ had both failed, by raising a perfect family—so I was taught. Sun Myung Moon was the one who would succeed where Christ had failed. We believed that he and his wife were the True Father and Mother. Well, who would credit it? I thought; I never realised that before! What a privilege to follow and serve him!

During the workshop, I kept hearing the words 'indemnity' and 'subjugation', which involved long fasts and cold showers, supposedly to ensure a good future and to overcome Satan and his temptations. There was no element of asking forgiveness and seeking God's grace to protect us from harm.

Spirits seemed to play a very big part in the teaching. Gary, one of the participants, prayed that the 'sleepy spirits' would enter him so that they would not distract young converts from the seminars, and there was talk of the spirits being 'playful' and 'harmless'. One of the other participants on the course claimed he had seen spirits in his room. 'I told them to go, in the name of Sun Myung Moon, and they left through the window,' he said.

One evening we went to a spiritist church meeting, where a medium was speaking. The first person the medium picked out was me! 'I've got a message for you, but you need to speak out,' she said. It was a very vague message from someone called John—it could have been anybody. Spirit beings play a major part in the teachings of the Unification Church. They are also very sympathetic towards Satan.

For 29th January 1978, a couple of weeks into the course, my diary entry reads: 'Richard gave us lectures. I listened to them without nodding off. Richard told us to go outside and ask God to speak to us through his creation. I noticed a pine cone lying on the ground, and concluded that it represented man's heart, closed up because of the coldness being shown towards it. We don't see birds doubting the existence of the air, or flowers doubting the existence of the rain; neither did there seem any reason to doubt God's existence.'

Seeing an old woman in tattered clothing walking in the neighbourhood, I thought how lonely she looked; as though no one in the whole world cared for her. It made me realise I had so much to offer, just by smiling at her and talking to her. I had so much real love and affection to offer—true love, not physical love. It was all so different from my previous hedonistic lifestyle. I was also becoming aware of many of the hurtful things I had said to people.

Towards the end of the workshop, after much role-playing, singing, worshipping, sketching, playing in the snow, praying and getting to know one another, I reached the point of finally accepting Sun Myung Moon as Messiah, the second Christ and third Adam. Every orthodox Christian would be appalled at this heretical concept, for the Moon is not the Son—but I felt wonderful!

'Heavenly Father has given us the opportunity to live in true happiness or hell, by giving us the choice between living for him or Satan,' I wrote. 'People can experience love between themselves, but this love is nothing compared with God's love for me and you. Satan has been attacking me spiritually by tempting me with lust. I really thought I couldn't live without it, which made me very depressed. I know that if I go back to Gail my girlfriend, and carry on in my old way it will completely destroy not only myself spiritually but also her, though she may not realise it.'

One day, we went fund-raising in Bromley High Street. A well-spoken middle-class lady and her daughter came up to me and took a *One World* leaflet that I was proudly selling. She tore it up in front of me and said that the Unification Church was of the devil. I was stunned! The leaders explained that this was simply 'persecution of God's chosen people'. I saw clearly then that unloving attitudes just convince sect members that they have 'the truth'. Only love and kindness can begin to show them that they are wrong.

My biggest crisis came when Gail turned up uninvited on the Livingstone House doorstep. You could have cut the atmosphere with a knife. She came in and we talked. At first I thought she was being quite understanding, but gradually she became more resentful and started repeating the bad things she had heard about the Unification Church. I told her I was enjoying myself a darn sight more than I had before, and she started bawling her eyes out. 'Please help me understand,' she cried, but she didn't want to listen, and in the end, I lost my temper and shouted at her. So much for all the pure and selfless love I claimed to be carrying!

We calmed down and I began to tell her about the *Divine Principle*. One of the other course participants also spoke with her and her resentment dropped drastically. As she left, she said desperately, 'If you find time to ring me you know where I am, because I know you're very busy.' In the end, I decided to let the heavenly Father guide me, otherwise I was going to get nowhere. Perhaps it's God's purpose that she join the Unification Church, I thought. She never did.

After the twenty-one days I signed up as a full-time member of the Unification Church and was promptly dispatched to Pearson Park, in Hull, with about a dozen other people. No 'hanky panky' was allowed between the sexes; such behaviour was regarded as spiritual suicide. There were, of course, sexual attractions; but these were never encouraged. In the end, Sun Myung Moon is the one who decides who is to be your marital partner.

My life in the 'Moonies' consisted largely of fund-raising, both in Hull and in other parts of Northern England. I sold copies of the Unification Church magazines, and asked people to spare money 'for missionary work'. Our mobile fund-raising team would target the high streets of a morning, the pubs of a lunchtime and back onto the high streets of an afternoon. A late lunch would be taken before going back to the pubs in the evening.

Manchester, Newcastle and parts of the Yorkshire Dales were all covered within a few weeks as we vigorously pursued our fund-raising. Hundreds of pounds were collected, though most of it was sent back to Lancaster Gate headquarters and the team was expected to live on a basic minimum. The wonderful meals we had been given during our training courses had been of high quality, but now we were expected to exist on stodge as poor as the insubstantial spiritual 'food'.

Soon I was down-at-heel and walking around in shabby clothing. When I pleaded for some of the money from the collection to replace my tatty clothing, I was told that I had to choose: if I wanted new trousers, I would have to go without food for a week! There was no way I was going to go without food, so eventually I received money for a new pair of trousers, although I was made to feel guilty for pursuing my own physical needs.

We were taught that the funds would be used to buy land in America, where God's kingdom on earth would be set up, governed by Sun Myung Moon. The vulnerable young people in our team all seemed to have stories of rejection and emotional hardship in their lives. We were all in pursuit of our own identity, seeking a permanent home where we could truly be ourselves. Once, we went to clean up a scruffy piece of land which had been turned into a rubbish tip—but only after ensuring that there would be plenty of coverage from the local newspaper. It was simply a way of making inroads into the confidence of the suspicious community. We sought to befriend local families, and to have them join our organisation and accept Sun Myung Moon as their Messiah. I remember the freezing cold evenings we spent trudging around houses giving away back issues of our magazines. At most doors, our reception was as cold as the weather. People were extremely cautious.

I disliked Hull from the beginning, and my dislike grew with my experiences there. I was sharing a house with people from Jamaica, Finland, Scandinavia and all over the world. We had nothing in common and no shared interests outside our commitment to the Unification Church. I was zealous in my fund-raising and proselytisation for the organisation. We believed that we had to reach the whole of Britain with the *Divine Principle* before 1981.

While in York, I spoke to a prominent Christian leader and remarked how sad it was that, since we all loved God, there could be no dialogue between the Unification Church and other denominations. In tranquil Durham I turned my hand to street preaching—in the driving snow!—protesting about churches selling books and coffee on a Saturday afternoon, which I regarded as very worldly. 'The church is God's place of prayer!' I shouted. 'Look how it has become a place of money and commerce!' I attempted to echo Christ's righteous anger when he threw the money changers out of the temple.

Another time, I used a sketchboard and easel in open air evangelism. After nervously writing on the board, I turned around and discovered that my efforts had attracted about a dozen spectators. Terrified, I explained what I thought to be the gospel to this tiny crowd, grateful for the support of other Unification Church members.

Once, we received a visit from a high-ranking couple in the organisation—Dennis and Dorothy Orme. At that time they were the Unification Church's British leaders, and we were so worried that they would think the house unclean, that we even scrubbed the top of the lavatory cistern. I asked Dennis for a lift down into town to continue with my fund-raising. A terrible hush fell over my colleagues who expected me to be reprimanded for such 'up-front' behaviour, but Dennis was very happy to drop me off at a prominent place with plenty of potential 'donors'.

As we drove into town, I shared with him the conversation I had had in York about inter-denominational dialogue. He was impressed that I had stood up so clearly for 'the faith'.

'I'm going for some fish'n'chips now,' he said. 'Would you like to join me?' Over our tasty cod and greasy chips, I asked him whether the stories I had heard about Sun Myung Moon were true—that he eats raw fish as a sign of humbleness. We both thought it was a load of old rubbish! This conversation gave me a link with one of the Unification Church's senior officials and I thought I was making headway in becoming a respected figure within the organisation.

Yet people I met on the streets continually told me that the organisation was dangerous. In America, I was told, people joined the 'Moonies' and were never heard from again. 'It's a sinister organisation,' I was told. I wanted to disbelieve it, but so many different people said the same. They pointed out a news story which told how the Unification Church had lost a libel case and landed itself with hundreds of thousands of pounds in court costs.

Questions were forming in my mind. Where does all this money we've been collecting actually go? Dennis Orme had explained patiently that it was all used for the development of the kingdom of God on earth. 'If someone gives just one penny towards our *One World* leaflets, that penny will count in his favour when he dies.'

I wasn't so sure.

I followed up one potential convert—a disabled person who had been brought to the centre by a female Japanese member—and was told by my group leader that he was 'bringing in bad spirits' and should be asked to stay away from our church centre. I was devastated! That attitude seemed so alien to the gospel I had been taught as a child at Sunday school.

This man, who had changed his name by deed poll to Bruce Lee, after his martial arts idol, was a badly hurt young man disillusioned with life. A few years after his rejection by the Unification Church, he was convicted as 'the Hull arsonist'. He was found guilty of squirting petrol through pensioners' letter boxes and throwing a match in afterwards. I believe he is still in a secure institution.

Gradually, the contradictions between theory and practice began to niggle at me, and to erode my confidence. We were taught not to feel bad towards the other members and try to avoid them but to talk through our negative feelings with them. The result, however, was not reconciliation but rather antipathy and resentment.

I had become an emotional mess, in an oppressive and authoritarian regime. It was forbidden to challenge the absolute authority of a leader—they could get away with blue murder and no one could question their power. A student in our house burned all his course notes shortly before his final examinations, as a 'sign of obedience' to

Sun Myung Moon—but no one in the Unification Church batted an eyelid. I was appalled.

Then I found myself sexually attracted to Sally, a local woman. She was attracted to me too! She came to me discreetly one day and said, 'There is a book I want to show you, which Viv has given me.' Viv was one of the young women in the church. At her home, Sally showed me a sexually-explicit book about a lesbian couple and explained that Viv had made overt sexual overtones towards her. She had stayed overnight once, and had tried to climb into bed with Sally.

We had talked for a little while, when a knock came at the door. I froze. Sally went to the door and found two of the bigger lads from the Unification Church standing there, calling my name. I knew that they believed that it was wrong to encourage someone to leave the Unification Church. I heard it taught that it is better to kill a person rather than let them leave, because in killing them their eternal salvation, that would otherwise be lost, can be preserved.

In fear and trepidation, I stayed 'holed up' at Sally's house for three nights, inevitably sleeping with her. We had a short but passionate physical relationship, which led to my rapid exit from the Unification Church. There was a church car parked outside for several nights, and 'Moonies' looking all over the place for me, asking people if they had seen me.

When the coast was clear, I got out of the house and headed for the motorway, intent on hitch-hiking down to London. Once back in the 'big smoke' I went around to see Dennis Orme and I confronted him about the book which Viv had given to Sally. Orme assured me that Viv was now over her 'little problem'; she was apparently not approaching other girls in the Church. It was clear that he knew all about her lesbian tendencies, which she had obviously had for some time, though he believed that the attempted physical expression of these feelings had been a 'one-off' occurrence.

'If you leave the Unification Church now,' Orme said, 'I believe you will be back within six months.' Then what? 'You will be put on probation for twelve months, on a mobile fund-raising team, an MFT, as a penance.' Those I had seen on MFT had looked like zombies. It was a frightening prospect.

Now I was on the outside, my former colleagues in the Unification Church offered me pity, and rebuked me for 'intellectualising' the problems I had. Yet I knew that I could never go back. If Sun Myung Moon was the Messiah, why did he allow his followers to behave in this deplorable and capricious way?

Elements of what they taught would be acceptable to the vast majority of Christians; here, I've only emphasised the differences. The cults don't tell a complete pack of lies; what they teach is substantially true to the Bible, with a few lies of their own thrown in. But unfortunately it doesn't take much poison to ruin a meal, and all cults destroy the goodness of the truth with a sprinkling of lies.

For example, the 'Moonies' use strong light and darkness allegories which stem from the *yin* and *yang* of eastern philosophy with its distorted dualism. There are also strands of teaching which urge people to see God in nature, which is pantheism. For the Unification Church, the supreme being is not a truly personal God in the way that orthodox Christians see him. Nor is Christ the Son of God. For them, the Son is eclipsed by the Moon . . .

The Unification Church is also fanatically anti-communist and Steven Hussan (ex-Moonie) says in his book *Combatting Cult Mind Control* (Park Street Press): 'I remembered hearing Moon say that if North Korea invaded South Korea, he would send American Unification members to die on the front line, so that Americans would get inspired to fight another land war in Asia.'

Mass suicide tragedies are not new to the cults. Years ago, members of the People's Temple in (Jim) Jonestown, Guyana, and more recently the Davidic Cult in Waco, Texas and the Swiss-based order of the Solar Temple, all 'sacrificed' themselves. Such is the power of cult mind control, and it is scary to think it could have been me . . .

Several people whom I had known in the 'Moonies' wrote to me expressing similar feelings to those that I was experiencing. Others continued to 'love bomb' me, hoping that I would return repentant to the fold. I was accused of committing 'spiritual suicide', but it would have been suicide to have stayed in such a repressive and unwholesome environment.

Like a drowned rat, my tail between my legs, I went back to stay with my dad in Romford for a while. Then I went back to Hull, staying in lodgings and continuing my relationship with Sally. I was not in love with her, but we were very fond of each other and I think we needed each other. After a time, however, I found it difficult to know when she was telling the truth.

On one occasion while I was with her, she went off with another man. She explained that she couldn't handle the relationship with me. When I went back to London to get a job, the relationship lapsed again and she started up with a third man.

I received a sympathetic letter from Gary, my former colleague—who had avoided being married by Sun Myung Moon at one of his mass weddings when he left with a female member from Finland and married her there soon after. Though they still considered Moon to be the Messiah, passionately believing that any problems were caused because the Messiah's teaching was being misrepresented. It was a belief I was inclined to hold for myself for several months.

Even when one is convinced that a course of action is right, there are always nagging thoughts, worries and fears. Like people who leave Jehovah's Witnesses, after living in constant condemnation within a heretical movement, I was fearful of orthodox denominations, continuing to believe that they were representative of Satan, and not of God.

I wasn't going to be fooled again. From now on, I was through with Sun Myung Moon.

And with Jesus Christ.

4

Visions of Africa

Back in London, I quickly found gainful employment with British Telecom, who wanted to train me to become a telegraphist. I was based at their Farringdon office, where I began a chapter in my life of which I am not proud.

In fact I now feel an overwhelming sense of shame for my past experience, even though in some cases I feel that I was the one being used; as John Lennon said in one of his songs, 'I once had a girl, or should I say, she once had me . . .'

In the telegram section, I could take my pick—married women as well as single. Many a girl was late with her period, and there were many anxious moments. I was lucky, too, not to pick up any diseases at that point. I always used condoms, but of course they are never one hundred per cent effective. The only way to avoid sexually-transmitted diseases, and unwanted pregnancy, is to avoid casual sex altogether. One lover wanted to marry me, fearing that she had fallen pregnant, though I had made it clear from the beginning that I was not looking for a long-term relationship.

'Is there anything I can do?' I asked her. 'It's none of your business any longer,' she told me firmly. She was off work for several months, but when she returned she was friendlier—though our affair was clearly terminated for good.

As an adopted child, I often wonder what would have happened if abortion had been such an easy option when my mother was carrying me. I might have been the victim of the abortion clinic myself, and never known what it's like to feel the wind in my face, or know any of the good things of life. I'm very opposed to abortion, and my feelings run deep.

At Christmas time I received presents from several different girls, all competing for my attention. I never bothered to buy them presents—though I did feel a bit embarrassed!—and before long, my name was 'mud' with one of the rebuffed girls, who began to talk about me behind my back. Once again, sex and drugs and rock'n'roll were the prominent features of my lifestyle. I certainly didn't want anything more to do with God. I once took a girl to St Paul's Cathedral one lunchtime, when she was expecting me to take her to a pub, but by and large, lust was the primary driving force in my life at that time.

I justified my attitude to women by shielding behind my oft-repeated claims that I wasn't looking for a long-term relationship. Often, women would feel that they could 'reform' me and ended up falling in love with me, but I would not commit to a permanent union or even a long-term relationship.

My technique was often to get a woman to talk about herself, her innermost feelings and experiences. Even then, I had good counselling skills, which I was happy to abuse. Many times, I would get women to discuss their views on life or religion. I knew that people often think that this person to whom they have been able to pour out their soul is the love of their life, their true soul mate. None of those women were ever really able to get me to open up about myself; none of them ever got to know the real 'me'. Perhaps they didn't want to; reality can shatter illusions.

My motives were hopelessly mixed in an exotic cocktail. I was genuinely interested in their opinions, because I remained totally fascinated by spirituality, even after getting my fingers burned by the 'Moonies'. It was only the established church that I rejected, in favour of anything mystic and esoteric. At the same time, I feared rejection myself from the women I seduced, suffering from a subconscious fear of long-term relationships in case I was the one to be hurt when they came to an end.

It doesn't last, of course. Anyone thinking of emulating my lifestyle had better watch for the consequences. If I'd begun my promiscuous lifestyle a few years later, I would probably have ended my days blind and emaciated in an AIDS hospice. I knew what I was doing, but I couldn't stop. I was trapped in a mindset where my own pleasure seemed the only solid thing in the world; the only thing worth pursuing.

Women wondered what there was about me which attracted other girls like insects into my web. I slept with women I didn't even find attractive, simply because they were available and through my intoxicated eyes they appeared to be 'not arf bad'! The permissive society was in full swing; I was gleefully swinging with it, and damn the consequences. The flipside of the permissive coin—single mothers with four or five children, often by different fathers—was an aspect that simply didn't concern me. The crop that might spring from my wild oats didn't figure on my agenda.

I wanted to get out of Britain. As a child, I had always dreamed of going to Africa. Now, whenever I saw a nature programme on television about the African continent, the wanderlust came back to me.

I had just turned twenty-one when, on returning from a short holiday in Ibiza with some old school friends, I discovered increased anxiety and mounting pressure at work. The telegram service was being made redundant as privatisation beckoned. Though I had always thought there were too many supervisors in my department—too many chiefs and not enough Indians!—the streamlining of the organisation and the fear of redundancy were stressful to everyone.

By October 1981, after two years at British Telecom, I had managed to raise enough money to make a long overland journey to the continent of my dreams. In the classified pages of *Private Eye* magazine, I found a six-month expedition advertised, for about £650 inclusive. The combination of circumstances conspired for me to hand in my notice and to exercise my itchy feet on the trip of a lifetime. The vast continent of Africa beckoned! Like Moon River, I was off to see the world, and there seemed such a lot of world to see.

At Charing Cross railway station one autumn morning, I met Scott Jalowski, a brash American who was one of the expedition members. I later learned that Scott had taken an instant and irrational dislike to me because of the colour of my rucksack. 'What sort of a jerk has a red rucksack?' he thought.

By some weird coincidence, I bumped into an old girlfriend at the station—Gail, whom I had once courted for about a year, prior to joining the 'Moonies'. Though she had since married, she seemed still to carry a deep hurt, and she smiled awkwardly as we chatted for a while. She was certainly more friendly than Scott, who sat as far as possible from me on the boat train!

We headed across to the continent, meeting up with the ten or so other members of the expedition—the exact number varied as people dropped out en route, and as new people came on board. We were a cosmopolitan party of both sexes and many nationalities, though mainly Australians and New Zealanders. Liz, one of the Australian girls, cut loose with a stream of expletives when the truck that was to be our transport to Africa was a couple of hours late. Chris, the main organiser, finally arrived—sitting in the front of an ex-Army truck laden with camping gear and cheap cooking utensils.

Chris, Sue and Scott travelled with us, but a second contingent, mainly from the Netherlands, was due to set out in another truck a few days later, and various rendezvous were expected during the trip. It was comforting to know that there would be a second vehicle nearby in the event of possible disaster.

We drove down through France and Switzerland to the toe of Italy, picking up some Swiss expeditionaries in Geneva. Then we crossed to Sicily uneventfully before proceeding over the Mediterranean to scorching Tunisia. There, the dazzling tropical sunshine made all the colours seem brighter, as though they had been washed and scrubbed. For ten days we savoured our first taste of Africa—camped beneath palm trees on the sweltering beach, waiting for our visas, before proceeding on to Algeria, a former French colony with a population of twelve million. Like French Legionnaires, we put our previous humdrum existence behind us.

We were sitting having a meal in the roasting Tunisian heat when one of my companions turned to me and said, 'Don't look now, but there's a camel coming through the restaurant!'

I think that was the first time it dawned on us that the ways of Africa were not the same as those of provincial Blighty. This was the beginning of many amusing encounters with vibrant cultures that simply didn't do things in the same fashion as we do in England, and our primary encounter with people of different mindsets and attitudes.

Here, the markets sold food stuffs we'd never set eyes on before, like yams, plantains, cassava and sweet potatoes.

Ducks, pigs and chickens wandered around the stalls of colourful cottons and striped djellabas in the market-place, while the aroma of exotic spices hung in the air.

Several of us bought colourful kaftan coats to try to merge in with the swarthy populace—though of course we still stood out like sore thumbs—the only people in the country clad in gaudy garb which owed more to the hippy movement than to the clothing taste of the average Algerian.

By this stage I was as brown as a berry. I looked so native that, for a joke, I accosted a respectable looking English tourist in the steaming marketplace and asked him in broken English whether he wanted to score some top-quality hashish! He responded with a shocked expletive and rushed away in horror at my childish humour.

Gradually some match-making began to take place within our intrepid band of travellers. I was not bothered in the slightest that I didn't get paired off myself—I really didn't fancy any of the women in our party, and the feeling seemed to be mutual.

We stopped off at a reptile farm, and also saw a few mangey lions in what seemed to be the equivalent of a rest home for geriatric animals. Another traveller signed up to join the party as we sped on past lush olive groves, through the local camel markets, and past butchers' shops where camel necks were hung up as a popular delicacy. I'm sure they tasted better than our staple diet of salty sardines, several tins of which we disposed of by donating them to a party of nomadic Tuaregs. Driving over the rolling Sahara sand dunes kissed with fire, sprinkled with an occasional acacia tree, we decided from then on to sample the local food, instead of trying to survive on the unappetising stuff with which the expedition organisers had supplied us.

The desert was a desolate, barren land, populated by thin cattle shuffling around far-flung water holes in the dry heat, with a few nomads eking out a living from the naked sand.

The desert people reminded me of the spice seekers in Frank Hubert's sci-fi classic, *Dune*, desperately conserving their precious water, and longing for a deluge that would never come. Bleak wastelands stretched to the north as far as the eye could see, while to the south I beheld the dramatic Hoggar mountains. We would set out before the scorching sun made travel unbearable, across the endless sea of sand dunes, burnished to the colour of gold by the fiery heat. As the day went on we would cover ourselves from the direct rays of the burning sun, now climbing above us as we raced towards the low mountain range. There, with the wind blowing like crazy—and night falling rapidly as we reached the foothills—we ate our evening meal dreaming of meat as we consumed our boiled vegetables.

The Hoggar mountains (sometimes spelt *Ahaggar*) are a sandstone range, cut by the restless wind into bizarre shapes, like natural sculptures. Welcomed only by a few snakes, we pitched camp for the night, glad to have safely crossed the largest desert on our planet. The cloudless sapphire sky began to darken as the night winds howled and the stars came out. The perspiration drenched my shirt and the soft sand still burned hot, but it would rapidly cool as night came on.

The Sahara desert was an apt metaphor for my own life really, though I didn't realise it at the time . . . .

We were a cowboy outfit, but it was the best cowboy outfit and a splendid time was guaranteed for all. We followed no strict itinerary and, if we broke down for a few days somewhere, it didn't matter much. The natives were friendly, and we soon became accustomed to the local booze wherever we turned up. We were grateful not to be part of one of the other expeditions we encountered, where holiday-making seemed to be run on the same lines as a military campaign.

There were some personality clashes among many of the adventurers on our truck, and a few departed for home unhappily. One guy, a law student from Australia, got right up everyone's nose, though I never had any trouble with him myself. One of our intrepid group members, 'Scott of the Sahara', rubbed many up the wrong way—particularly in the middle of the trackless desert when he decided to wash his hair with most of what remained of our precious water supply!

I had no problem blending in with the general hedonistic vibe of the expedition. I was always surprised when people couldn't hack the trip, because I was having the time of my life.

Eventually, our numbers became so depleted that we combined with the equally diminished Dutch expedition and continued as one party, and after that we all got on famously for the rest of the trip.

By the time we reached Cameroon, the countryside began to get greener. The French-speaking people were friendly, and they certainly knew how to have a good time. The country seemed to me to be full of bars, each with a powerful PA system outside, blasting out contagious dance rhythms. These sleazy bars were packed with men drinking beer straight from the bottle—only sissies used glasses. I was nearly deafened by the volume of the wicked dance music blaring into the night from those enormous speaker columns.

In a former French colony, Central African Republic—tropical and verdant with its myriad shades of green—I stumbled upon a meat market, where dismembered monkey meat, cooked over a charcoal fire, was on sale. The women saw the expression of horror on my face, and baited me by holding out a charred piece of monkey for me to taste. My tongue gagged in my throat at the prospect. The more I threw up my hands in horror at the sight of dismembered arms and legs, the more the women laughed at me, particularly when I threw up my breakfast in the gutter. Give me a McDonald's Big Mac any day!

One of my fellow travellers—there were about a dozen of us at this point—got drunk one night and rolled back to our campsite with a prostitute in tow. Not wanting to 'perform' in front of us all, he took her back to his tent, and promptly fell asleep. When he woke up in the morning, his sleeping partner wanted payment for spending the night with him. He refused to pay on the grounds that he had been 'drunk and incapable', so she went off and came back with a big bouncer. An equally big argument ensued, during which the prostitute took off her wig and threw it on the floor in disgust! My fellow travellers all sided with the bald whore, one of them deliberately mistranslating her French to ensure that our impotent Romeo ended up paying three times over the odds for the service he had never received.

I met a keen Bob Marley fan in one of the seedy bars—at that time, the great world music star had scarcely been a month in his Kingston mausoleum—and quickly befriended him. He showed me where to buy skewers of meat that didn't come from monkeys. We smoked a few joints and had a whale of a time. On New Year's night (1981–2) we crossed the Ubangui river—and the international frontier—into Zaire.

In tropical Zaire, two of my companions had their money stolen by a sneak thief who cut open the canvas of their tent to relieve them of their valuables. The matter was reported to the local police, who dragged off one of the local young people into a nearby mud hut with a thatched top, where we heard his terrified screams as he was beaten. We believed that the African police had found a scapegoat and thrashed him, virtually torturing him, in order not to lose face in front of us Europeans. The politics of many of these African countries was way 'off the wall'; they were virtually police states.

The Zaire leg of the trip was particularly rich in events: 'This vast country epitomises everyone's archetypal image of Africa—endless jungles, enormous rivers, wild animals, wild people, mountains, volcanoes and the most diabolical transport system you will come across anywhere in the world,' Geoff Crowther says of this vigorous and untamed land in his grassroots travel guide *Africa on the Cheap*.

My Australian friend Grant and I decided to imbibe the local colour by leaving the truck—we needed to exercise our legs and the 35 kilometre walk seemed ideal. We walked through villages, orange groves and rubber plantations. A party of students we encountered, who were hiking a dozen miles home from college, couldn't understand why anyone would want to walk when they could ride. The concept of choosing to ride or walk was lost on them, because they had never experienced such choices themselves.

'Are you a Christian, Gordon?' one of them asked me out of the blue once we had got to know one another on the walk. He was shocked when I shook my head.

'Please tell me that you are a Christian,' he begged, unable to accept that I had no interest in organised religion. He had been indoctrinated by Catholicism, and probably believed that because I wasn't a practising Christian I was bound for hell, according to the theology he had probably imbibed with his mother's milk, never studying the Scriptures for himself.

We were walking along a dirt track up to a mud hut when we were offered delicious palm wine and fruit by a friendly local man, who refused to accept payment for it. A bit further on we had a bit more palm wine, and smoked a bit of dope. This was the life.

Soon I was literally up the river without a paddle, on the deck of a ramshackle river boat, churning up the Congo river—a change from the monotony of bumpy land transport. The food was crude; for one meal, I found nothing but a large fish head sitting on top of my meagre bowl of rice. Once, a canoe pulled up alongside and the local fishermen offered me a bowl of edible wood grubs as an alternative to my brainy catfish. It was all part and parcel of the experience, so I decided not to complain too much.

People seemed to appear from nowhere out of the endless rain forest with trinkets for sale as our boat passed. I got blind drunk with a squad of local soldiers who had taken a liking to me and smoked so much dope that I got along splendidly with anyone and everyone—missing out on the rough rides, it seemed, because I felt as though I was floating six inches above everything most of the time.

When Scott bought a pet monkey at a local market, no one batted an eyelid—until it became apparent that the monkey was partial to the cheap marijuana we all carried with us. The monkey began stuffing marijuana seeds into its mouth and got so high he couldn't climb anything without falling off. We called him Guy, the Junky Monkey.

My celibacy didn't last long in these conditions. One of the Dutch girls kept whining to her best friend about how much she missed the boyfriend whom she had left behind. When we hit it off, she desperately tried to keep our intimacy secret from her friend, whom she feared would be angry with her hypocrisy.

That was the sex and drugs. The rock'n'roll came from the handful of Van Morrison tapes we had with us, which we nearly wore out from constant playing of the celtic band's soulful anthems. Three members of the party had brought guitars with them, and they played non-stop jam sessions for much of the trip. I have happy memories of improvising stupid lyrics, or singing rock'n'roll standards, to the blues riffs driven by guitars and make-shift bongos as we sprawled around a camp fire in the tropical night. Sometimes it was difficult to know whether to let go of the girl or the joint in order to pick up the bottle of booze. . . .

On the border of Zaire and Rwanda, I went on a hunting

trip with a tribe of pygmies. Small? They were minute! We paid the local government officials a flat fee to join the hunting party, and set off through the dense rainforest. The little people had no problem ducking and diving beneath the tropical undergrowth, but we Europeans were constantly smacked in the face by exotic foliage, as we tripped the light fantastic over creepers and vines. Lanky Hank banged his head on a few branches. Rare birds with colourful plumage flapped out of our way, strange lizards scuttled around our feet, and enormous dragonflies flew at our faces.

To show their hunting prowess, our tiny friends set nets and drove the wild deer into them in a scene straight from a David Attenborough documentary. Hank was sitting on a rotten tree stump, imagining the succulent aroma of roast venison, when a shout went up from one of the pygmies. He advanced on Hank with a fierce expression and a razor-sharp machete raised in anger. Hank jumped up, and the pygmy decapitated the leathery snake that had been sliding silently underneath him. . . .

Though we had already paid up front for the trip, our diminutive guides decided that they were not going to take us back to camp unless we coughed up some more money! Negotiations were delicately conducted in broken pygmy and pidgin English. Roughly translated, they were saying, 'Pay up or find your own way back! P.S. There are some nasty head-hunters in this neck of the woods.' They also demanded a flat fee for each photograph we took of them. Commercialism is alive and well, deep in the Zaire undergrowth. Who needs poison darts and blowpipes when you have this much business acumen? They'll be selling shrunken heads in velvet-lined presentation boxes next! You had to laugh.

Past the towering Ruwenzori range, poetically known as 'the mountains of the moon', over the equator and on through Rwanda, and so into Tanzania. Here there seemed to be large numbers of cripples begging. It was heartbreaking. Though the people lived in rags, their mud huts were spotlessly clean, 'vacuumed' with banana leaf brushes. I was struck by the dignity of these noble people.

We crossed the Serengeti, a vast savannah filled with wildebeest, zebras, gnus, giraffes, lions and elephants—like a television wildlife programme unfolding before my eyes—only I was in the middle of it! There seemed to be millions of tropical animals migrating across the fertile grasslands. We went down into the massive Ngorongoro crater, and saw the pink haze of thousands of flamingos parading around a broad lake, eyed up by lions, cheetahs and tigers, as rhinoceroses and hippopotami wallowed in their waterholes.

With reckless bravado we got out of our truck and went for a close-up of this extraordinary panorama of African wildlife, soaking up the atmosphere. Hyenas munched on a carcass, vultures hovered like waiters for the chewed remnants. I tasted the rains, felt the hot earth beneath my feet, the tropical breeze in my face, and I was lost in my wanderlust. This was the life I wanted to last for ever.

In a bar one night, I ended up on stage singing some Bob Marley songs backed by a vibrant twelve-piece band. Next day, I met up with some of the players for a few smokes of ganga weed. A whore slid in from the brothel next door, and ended up eating the soggy roach (the discarded stub of our joint). 'We waste nothing around here,' she said. Aghh! I was disgusted.

Still, a nifty black market currency exchange with some canny Asian immigrants soon made me a wealthy man in Tanzanian currency. The Asians were clearly the driving business force in the country at that time, before the expulsions in nearby Uganda made them flee for fear of similar events overtaking them.

On through Tanzania and into Kenya we ventured—

snow-capped Kilimanjaro, Africa's tallest peak, in the far distance. We arrived in Nairobi for a brief stay, then took off down the coast, renting a house on the beautiful Lamu island, whose silver beaches make it a hippie haven. There were never any traffic accidents there because the only car on Lamu belonged to the local governor. Eventually, we left this tropical paradise and headed back to Nairobi, where we stayed in cheap accommodation, and frequented the bars of all the posh hotels. We had a whale of a time.

In some parts of Kenya, there seemed to be more Asians than Africans; they had migrated there in the forties, after partitioning in India. In one particularly poor Asian ghetto, we found a place called The Green Bar which seemed to be the centre of all the illegal activity in the neighbourhood. This notorious place of prostitution and violence, where everyone drank beer and bootleg liquor straight from the bottle, rapidly became our home-from-home. It was certainly a long way from the Unification Church!

Nairobi is a luxurious and affluent city, but one surrounded by the shacks of a shanty town where poverty reigns. I tried to blot these out as our whole party went off to the coastal resort of Malindi, where we spent days on end sunbathing naked on the beaches, enjoying the liberated atmosphere. There was a fatalistic nagging at the back of my mind, though, that made me think that everything was so good something had to go wrong.

Then it happened.

That was the night we all got blind drunk, and were pulled up by the two gun-toting policemen on our way back to the cheap hotel to which we had moved. And the policemen decided to search us . . .

Of course, I'd forgotten all about the stash of 'wacky backy' I'd been given earlier, until they pulled it out of my pocket and confronted me with it! A summer season in prison looked likely as they took me back to the cells, and I sobered up rapidly. One police officer began shouting. They made me take off my shoes and socks and threw me in a squalid cell with two prisoners who were little more than children. The non-stop shouting continued for most of the next day. A young girl who had been in the next cell was badly treated by one of the guards, who threw her to the ground and screamed abuse at her.

I had no inkling of what Kenya's attitude to drugs would be. Memories of the film *Midnight Express* haunted me, with the prospect of months of confinement without trial, followed by twenty years' imprisonment in a strange country—a horrific prospect which grew more frightening by the hour. *Somebody get me out of here!*

Eventually I was hauled up before the local magistrate who regarded me with disdain. By some mistake of translation, the charge of possessing five grammes of marijuana for my personal use had become one of trafficking in five *kilograms* of dope. I suddenly felt like a big time drug baron, awaiting the death sentence.

Luckily the mistake was soon sorted out, and the judge's black hat failed to appear. Clearly the 'beak' regarded me as no more than a petty criminal. I was fortunate that two of my travelling companions, Grant and Jean-Claude, came to court with enough money to pay the stiff fine that was handed down from the bench. What a relief! I was free again!

My friends had chipped in to pay my fine, but my financial reserves were seriously depleted and a depression had started to settle over me like a funeral shroud. I'd had a wickedly bad experience, which dissuaded me from ever smuggling drugs—or anything else—but otherwise I had learned nothing from it. My only comfort, incongruously enough, was from a satirical book by Spike Milligan, whose irreverent look at life frightened away some of the doom and gloom.

Sue, a travelling companion who was like a sister to me, expressed concern about the way I had become so rattled and on edge. I shouted abuse at one of my best mates simply because he started reading a newspaper I had bought before I had read it myself. I was shocked, too, by the 'sexploitation' of children that I realised was happening in the country, judging by the plight of the sexually-active young children who had shared my cell. It had taken my own temporary incarceration to bring home to me the reality of the poverty, degradation and suffering which made up the other side of life in this vibrant country whose sudden unpredictability had sent me reeling.

This adverse climax of the trip made me unbearable company for a while. Diving in Malindi helped clear my head, and the contrast of some obnoxious Canadian children who demanded more and more from their father, while the poor local children with their bottoms hanging out of their trousers had not a care in the world, set me thinking. The sight of legless beggars scurrying around on little carts, challenged me about east-west inequalities and my own position in the world, but didn't inspire me to do anything about it. It took a few more beers to set me on my feet again.

As I prepared to return to Britain, I realised that the travel bug had bitten me deeply. Just as Guy the monkey had been 'turned on' by dope, I had become a travel junky. Though deep inside, my heart yearned to find a place to settle, which it could truly call 'home', on another level I felt that the thrill of the journey was more important for the time being.

Perhaps one day I would find the peaceful pastures where my soul could be at ease. It wouldn't be a house with roses around the door, where I could sit with my pipe and slippers, but I hoped that one day I would discover what 'home' really meant for someone like me, who couldn't settle down into one steady relationship, do without my daily 'fix' of dope, stay in one job for any length of time, or even stay in the same country for long without the wanderlust leading me on new journeys.

What was I searching for? Perhaps my 'real self'. Or perhaps a true father who would be my father for ever, and who wouldn't put me up for adoption into another man's home. Perhaps a person who would love me for myself without asking for ties and binds which I didn't feel ready to make.

Little did I know that such a person was looking out for me, and had been waiting patiently for all my life. For now, the travelling seemed more important than the destination. The road was calling me and offering more in return than any person, place or career could hope to provide.

PART TWO

The Long Way Home

5

In the Mystic East

I was skint! I had to sell my camera in Nairobi to raise the airfare to fly Aeroflot back from Kenya.

Every seasoned traveller knows that Aeroflot is about the cheapest airline in the world; it's based in Russia, and the planes are practically held together with string. Flying with weight-lifting air hostesses who looked like Arthur Mullard in drag was quite an experience. They kept waking us up to feed us; it seemed that every time I nodded off, I was shaken awake to find a plate of caviar pushed in front of me. There were no allocated seats; the whole experience was like hopping on a bus.

At the stopover in Moscow we kept being shuffled between planes till the crew found one they liked. After spending so long in the tropics, the bitter Russian winter was particularly gruelling. I finally rolled back into rain-soaked Britain in April 1982.

From Heathrow, I took a train back to Romford to stay with my dad for a few days, and to tackle the problem of finding a job. Luckily Sue, my platonic pal from the expedition, knew of an apple farm down in Kent which needed workers, so I headed down to Maidstone for a three-month picking season. That was followed by a series of temporary jobs, with which I struggled to raise enough money for another foreign trip.

Back in Romford, I discovered that my sister Sharon's psychiatric illness had worsened and she was going through a crisis. Her condition led her to become totally self-absorbed, as she reverted to a helpless and extremely vulnerable individual, consumed by confusion, illusion and fear. However I tried to break through her alienation and communicate with her, she hardly batted an eyelid in response. When Dad had the flu, he pleaded with her to go round to the house and help him, but she refused point blank. Mentally ill people are often selfish and manipulative—the world has to revolve around them—but her attitude knocked him for six. In the end I made him some food and looked out for him, and once I showed that I cared—when his favourite child didn't—it completely changed his attitude towards me. This simple yet painful scenario proved to be a wonderful turning point, restoring respect to our relationship with one another. From that moment on, my dad and I were able to develop a proper father and son relationship. I helped him to put his life back together and to develop new interests. I took him along to a club for widows, widowers, divorcees and singles, and introduced him around. He got on with everyone like a house on fire, and quickly became Entertainment Manager organising various outings.

Though no one could replace Mother, he was desperately lonely and needed someone to share his life. At one point, it looked as though he would marry again, until his prospective spouse said that Sharon and I would no longer be welcome in the family home. Angrily, my dad retorted, 'No one tells me what to do, or says that my own kids are not welcome in my own home.' He showed her the door, and it was the last we saw of his 'new woman'.

My lovely fair-haired sister had been through a string of

relationships and lived in dozens of flats over the previous few years. Soon, though, she was back in our Romford home, albeit making frequent excursions to the Robin Hood pub in Barking—notorious, at that time, as a pickup place, where you could meet all sorts of characters searching for love and affection, each hoping that one night their prince (or princess) would come, pint of Tetleys in hand, to sweep them off their feet. If you were desperate for a partner, that's where you went. Sharon came back one night from this 'grab a granny' lonely hearts club proclaiming that true love had found her at last, and she had met her Prince Charming.

'He's wonderful. I'm moving in with him,' she announced, and a big scene ensued as Dad and I tried to persuade her to get to know the man a bit better first. There was no reasoning with her; she called a cab, loaded her belongings, and she was off. But a week later she came tearing back, crying her eyes out.

'He attacked me with a knife!' she wailed. One of my old mates, Trevor Bacon, was visiting me at the time, so we piled into his car and raced down to the local police station. Sharon told her story at great length while the officer listened patiently. As soon as she mentioned her erstwhile lover's name, his ears pricked up. No fewer than *six* police officers escorted her to Prince Charming's flat to retrieve her clothing and belongings. Sharon's 'prince', the police told us, had recently been released from Broadmoor, a secure hospital for the criminally insane. . . .

Dad was devoted to my sister and me, and I'm sure he would have loved me to have stayed at home and got married, but I was already married to the open road and the endless possibilities which the wide world offered for travel.

Israel beckoned to me, and I was soon standing in the baking sun once more. The palm trees of Tel Aviv looked lovely after all the boring apple trees I'd seen on the Kent farm. I'd made arrangements to meet Sue for an overland trip across the Sinai desert to Egypt, from where we were intending to go through the Sudan back to Kenya. At least that was the idea.

I spent an enjoyable two months living on a large kibbutz, working during the day and enjoying the nightlife around the swimming pool during the evening. My job as a 'kibbutznik' involved working in the dairy with these enormous cows fed on protein. A worker would come round to service the cows with a tube of bull's sperm and a pipette. Rather him than me, I thought. It was a messy business—and not much fun for the cow either!

Unfortunately I developed dermatitis due to the chemicals used to disinfect the cows' teats, and had to move to a less prestigious job, servicing the rooms of the volunteers as an odd job man. I was grateful not to be working out in the fields under the hot sun, or in the factory doing one of the many less pleasant jobs.

I found myself sharing a room with the only two Christians on the whole kibbutz, one Finnish and one American, so it was natural that several religious discussions ensued. These followers of Christ emphasised that the teachings about God I had received in the Unification Church were in serious error. 'The God depicted in *Divine Principle* is neither omnipresent nor sovereign in earth's affairs,' they said. 'Much of their teaching borders on the occult, and Mr Moon's ridiculing of Christ's death and resurrection is blasphemy of the highest order.' Moon was a poor substitute for Jesus Christ, I eventually had to agree; but the Unification Church had, for a while, given my life purpose in a way the established churches had never done. Who was really right? I just didn't know.

The Finnish guy came up to me once with a handful of plastic pellets in his hand. 'Even though most are white and pure, the little black ones are like sin in a person's life—they ruin the pure goodness,' he said, trying to evangelise me.

'Just back off,' I said. 'If you want to win me around to your Christian view, do it by loving me, not by forcing me. Your heavy-handed evangelism is just driving me crazy!' He apologised and went away.

A small group of us met occasionally to smoke a little dope. Little did we know that one of the volunteers was actually an undercover agent for the Israeli police. He informed on us and, though we weren't arrested, we were staggered at being forced to leave the kibbutz. We were good workers and felt sad that for such a small amount of weak marijuana we should be asked to leave.

Moshe, one of the friends I made on the kibbutz, invited me to stay with his family in a small flat for a few weeks while I tried a selection of employment opportunities; stuffing pillows for three days was a particularly tedious and thankless job. Moving on to dusty Jerusalem, I was lucky to get a job in an Indian restaurant—though I got the sack after a week.

I found details of a nearby Palm Hostel, which turned out to be run by young Christians, and I moved in there when life got too complicated even for me—sometimes it seemed that everyone I met either wanted to 'convert' me, or to sleep with me! I went to several religious services there, but I was still too disillusioned after my experience with the 'Moonies'. 'What do you do about girlfriends?' I asked one of the Christian lads. 'What about sex?' The aspect which most frightened me away from the religious life was the prospect of having to become celibate, and not being able to do as I wanted.

'It's difficult,' they admitted, 'but we have something more worthwhile at the end of the day.' Their faith sustained them through all temptation. Circumstances had conspired once more to offer me a choice, but this time I decided to choose *against* following Jesus Christ.

Sue was unable to meet me in Israel after all, so she sent me a letter and a rendezvous was arranged in Cairo. Like Moses in reverse, backtracking from the Promised Land, I crossed the border into Egypt and made my way to the Egyptian capital. I stayed in the dirtiest, filthiest hostel I have ever seen in my life, complete with giant cockroaches. Black market dealing and drug pushing were the norm—'Sure you don't want to buy some more hashish?' I was constantly asked—but fortunately some good travel information was also available.

Cairo was a hive of activity. One day, I scored some dope and ended up in a cinema watching *Star Wars*, pleasantly stoned. A fat boy next to me kept offering me peanuts and the blokes behind talked the whole way through the film, while various tradesmen came in periodically to sell glasses of tea. It was quite an event.

I stayed in Cairo for several weeks, trying to get a visa to go through Sudan. The fighting in south Sudan made the government reluctant to give visas, for fear of the international repercussions if a tourist should accidentally get shot. When Sue finally met up with me, we toured around Egypt visiting the pyramids and various far-flung oases. Then she went off to the coast, leaving me to collect my passport from the Sudanese embassy. I never did get the visa, so I regretted not going to the coast with Sue and the other friends we'd made.

The relationship with Sue remained platonic to the end. Most of the travelling girls I met were never looking for romance—they were simply after a good time. For them at least, it was true that 'girls just want to have fun'. But even on one-night stands, the level of conversation was often very deep, talking of God, life, the universe and everything.

Many people search for God in the mystic east and,

though finding him wasn't a high priority on my agenda, the quest for a genuine religious experience was an idea that flitted through my mind occasionally. I turned my sights towards the rising sun and began to consider travelling east again, into the heart of Asia.

It may seem a strange choice of route to get from Egypt to India, but the cheapest way I could find was to return to Israel, catch a boat to Greece, and then book a flight from Athens to Bombay!

In transit, I met a chap who was studying to be a priest, and I soon fell into deep conversation with him. He was very liberal in his theology, and quite confused, but he helped me to narrow down some of my own thoughts about religion as we spoke of God and worked through many spiritual issues; but my memories of the 'Moonies' again prevented me from becoming committed in any way to the views that he espoused. When I caught my flight, his words were still tumbling through my mind.

Jet-lagged, I landed in sprawling Bombay and found cheap accommodation with another new-found friend, Leo, whom I had met on the plane. His long hair tied back in a ponytail, and his long finger nails varnished black, made me think he was a free-spirited man—perhaps another traveller like myself. I knew little about India, but the west coast resort of Goa had always featured favourably in many travellers' tales told to me on my journeys; I thought I would give it a try, but getting there would take longer than I had anticipated. Though Leo was German, he had acquaintances in Hyderabad and invited me to join him there first, travelling by slow train beneath the scorching sun. When we arrived, I found that the countryside was beautiful and the drugs were cheap and strong, so a good time was had by all.

A few weeks later, we chanced to meet two women who had just returned from a Christian commune—an *ashram*, as religious communities are called in India—down near Pondicherry, in South India. Leo and I decided to check it out.

The sweltering heat at that time of year was unbearable, but the *ashram* itself was shaded by palm trees and felt very tranquil. Bede Griffiths was the leader of the *ashram*, and I spoke with him several times. He asked me where I was from and wanted to know what I was searching for, but first and foremost he warmly welcomed me to stay as long as I wished. A truly humble man, he possessed tremendous grace and presence. He was a spiritual man in every sense of the word.

During our second long meeting, I asked him about 'the blood of Jesus'. It was a concept which the Christians I had met in Israel had tried to explain to me, but I couldn't understand how the blood of a man who died a criminal's death two thousand years ago could have any significance to people living in the twentieth century.

His reply was, 'What *about* the blood of Jesus? It's hardly mentioned in the Bible. Why is it a big issue to you?' There was something about the concept of sacrifice which intrigued me, but I didn't know why. Perhaps I was confused by my memories of the strange occult teaching I had received in the Unification Church, or perhaps I was just being a bit thick, but I couldn't figure out what Christ's death was supposed to mean to me today.

God I accepted as my creator all along. I could relate to God better than I could relate to Jesus. I always felt that being committed to Jesus was very important, but was it 'right' for me? I thought not, because it clashed with my evolving New Age views. Christianity seemed to stress the basic sinfulness of man, and at that time I preferred the idea that we were all gods in the making, creating a perfect world for ourselves. It fitted in better with my lifestyle, so truth would just have to bend to my requirements. . . .

IN THE MYSTIC EAST

My stay at the *ashram* really made me think. I began to inquire into Confucius and Gautama the Buddha, and to delve deeper into eastern mysticism. I practised what was called Christian yoga, and engaged in long conversations with other members of the *ashram*. Like everywhere else in India, the cost of living was low and I was in no hurry to move on at first. But Leo eventually had to return to his job in Germany, and my own feet were soon getting itchy for the road.

When I felt that I had learned all that I was capable of digesting for the time being, I continued on my way—with a Belgian girl in tow, who was heading in the same direction, up to Varanassi. She proved an invaluable support whenever we had problems with the Indian transport system. I remember her verbally laying into the station manager at Madras about a confusion over train times. The manager was shocked and bemused by the way I appeared to be letting a woman do my speaking for me—an unusual occurrence in Indian society. He turned to me and said, 'Do you not speak English?'

'I *am* English!' I exclaimed. 'But I can't get a word in edgeways!' Eventually he found us a couple of sleeper berths for the first part of the journey. Though far from luxurious, they were at least tolerable. For the remainder of the two-day journey, we sat on hard wooden benches in second class—I think we'd have been more comfortable on the roof. By the time I reached Varanassi, on the banks of the Ganges, I was completely exhausted.

Like death warmed up we crawled off the train and made our way to a well-known travellers' lodge, where copious quantities of dope soon had me flat on my back catching up with some much-needed kip. We quickly discovered a local *bhang* shop—an official government dope house where this opiate-based narcotic could legally be purchased. *Bhang* itself resembled a sweet, a small round ball wrapped in paper. Various grades of hashish, opium and marijuana were also available in this junky's paradise.

I often went with groups of fellow travellers down to the *bhang* shop, returning with huge slabs of dope that would be shared among us each evening. We smoked the most extraordinary joints with fresh high-quality pot, rolled up into giant reefers the size of cigars! Stoned legless each evening, we staggered around many of the temples for which the city is famous.

There are more holy places in Varanassi than anywhere else in India—probably anywhere in the world. Many are sacred to the god Shiva, whose symbol—an enormous phallus—is kept constantly moist with filthy Ganges river water. Even in my condition, I could sense something very creepy about the spirituality oozing from such places. I felt heavy in my heart over what I could see of Asian spirituality.

Hinduism has several paths. The oldest, *karma yoga*, was originally a sacrificial system, but is now interpreted as 'doing good deeds'. *Jnana yoga* is very philosophical, requiring a guru or religious teacher, and is now indistinguishable from Mahayana Buddhism. *Bhakti yoga* is the most popular, and entails selfless devotion to one's chosen god. These routes, and others, are all designed to lead the soul out of the endless cycle of births (*samsara*), a belief which is at the very heart of the faith. Hinduism has been like a sponge, absorbing every new idea that comes along, and is now heavily steeped in arcane folklore.

Our hostel was next to a dank temple whose worshippers woke us each morning with the noisy din of their devotions. We were at the very heart of Hinduism, seeing the faith at its most popular level—and witnessing the superstition which undergirds its everyday practice. At other times, in the sweltering heat, we took boats along the cool river, upon whose banks the bodies of orthodox Hindus are cremated.

Soon it was time to move on again. Several days spent in Nepal, in the sleepy village of Pokhara, beside a lake nestled at the bottom of a tranquil valley, flew past in a smoky haze. Pokhara, apparently, was a place of pilgrimage for many Buddhists, and a place of extraordinary natural beauty. Overwhelmed, I spent three weeks trekking through the exquisite country, close to exotic Kathmandu, watching the green landscape change to brown and grey as we climbed higher into the cold clouds, past fortified medieval towns, through forests of fir and juniper, up and up to around eighteen thousand feet.

The Nepalese people seemed to work all hours of the day. In one guest house we stayed in, high in the mountains, it was the children who did all the cooking and cleaning. I saw the same very young but very worn out faces of many working children in India. It seemed that the Buddhism practised in Nepal made the people no happier than the Hinduism of South Asia. An undercurrent of sadness pervaded that lovely country, leaving me melancholy as I turned back towards the furnace heat of India.

One of my companions, Hans, had bought two hundred pounds' worth of jewellery in India, having been told that he could resell it in Nepal for a handsome profit. It didn't take us long to realise that the impoverished people were quite unable to purchase these trinkets at a price which would turn any profit.

Hans made his way back to the man who had sold him the baubles, in order to have some severe words with him. The shopkeeper pleaded poverty. 'I cannot repay the purchase price of the jewellery. What's the point in threatening me when I don't have the money?' he said. In the end, the jewellery was exchanged for items that Hans would find easier to sell when he returned to his native Germany.

Next stop was Agra, where we took a room in a hostel near to the Taj Mahal—definitely one of the seven wonders of the world in my eyes, especially at night when the rich marble seemed to glow with a translucent beauty. The awesome symmetry of the four sides—identical except for the front, where the entrance is located—with their ornate carvings and embellishments took my breath away. It was a magical experience, but one which left me wanting another one, and another, the way that purely worldly experiences often do with their impermanence.

While in Agra I witnessed the spectacle of a gang of boys setting upon a hog and pulling out great clumps of its hair to make hog hair brushes. You can imagine the pandemonium and the noise that the hog was making with its angry squealing!

So much of India seemed to retain echoes of colonial England that just walking around was like watching a living history lesson. The people were unfailingly pleasant and helpful, even after we reached Delhi in the middle of a heat wave that was too hot even for the seasoned residents. Having travelled through the Sahara desert and the African jungle, I thought I knew what heat was; but this was unbearable. It was the first time I experienced all the pores in my neck opening and water pouring out. Even the locals were finding it difficult; everyone was drinking colossal amounts of water in an attempt to prevent dehydration.

By now, my finances were once again getting low and I needed to get back home. Just as I had in Kenya, I sold my camera to get enough money to buy an Aeroflot flight back to London—but with nothing left to cover living expenses up till the plane left. Since the next flight was more than a week away, I was stuck without enough money. My only option was to try to get back via an overland route.

Fellow travellers suggested a route that I could afford and so I decided to give it my best shot, and set off homewards. First stop was Islamabad, in Pakistan, to collect a visa that would take me into the Shi'ite Muslim stronghold of Iran.

It was Ramadan when I reached Pakistan, but Islamic law permitted foreign travellers to be served with refreshment. When his staff began to attend to me, one shop keeper rushed up and refused my custom. 'You hypocrite!' I retorted. 'You'd rather see someone die in the street than give them a drink.' I had seen the bodies of the dead and dying in the gutters of India, and my words were loaded with particular venom. My outburst cost me dearly; I stubbed my toe and broke a nail on my way out. It was agony.

At a refugee camp for soldiers who had run away from the fighting in the Iran–Iraq war, I made friends with a well-educated telecommunications officer from Iraq. He believed Saddam Hussein was right and that they were fighting a just war. On the front line he had received a telex message that had come in garbled. He couldn't give the required order simply because he couldn't read it, but his friends told him that his life was in danger from Hussein's fanatical officers who would have him executed for this unavoidable failure. He had to get out. Days of furtive travel got him across the border, into Iran and on into Pakistan, where he could be safe; but then his water ran out.

'My God! What shall I do? Please help me!' He turned around and saw the distant shimmer of water. He filled his bottle at an oasis and was saved.

The second time he ran out of water, he cried out again. Looking up, he saw in the desert a jeep-load of rebels coming towards him, armed to the teeth. They were going to kill him, but he told them he knew the leader of their band. 'We will take you to him,' they said, 'but if you are lying, and you don't know him, we will kill you.' He did indeed know the rebel chief, who then helped him to reach the refugee camp.

I had no reason to disbelieve his story. God is a God of liberation, who helps people, I thought. Islam may not be the best way to God but, even in my state of spiritual ignorance, I could see no reason why God in his grace should not have heard the man's prayers and helped him.

Armed with a fifteen-day transit visa, I made my way up to the Iran border in a very beautifully decorated bus, but one which gave the bumpiest ride imaginable. There were bits of metal sticking in my leg and big bumps under my seat. I tried travelling on the roof for a while, but you had to be constantly on the lookout for overhead wires. The second bus I boarded, on the other side of the border, was a European coach with proper seats and air conditioning. Sinking into the luxury of the upholstered seats I was in ecstasy!

I stopped off at an Iranian hotel with a German couple I'd met and we were soon 'skinning up' a joint and—like veteran hippies—taking long whiffs of the sweet smoke. It was only later that I found out that Iran takes as dim a view of narcotics as it does of alcohol. Iranians can get their hands cut off for less, and I believe the usual penalty for foreigners is a public flogging!

We were beginning to 'chill out' on the strong marijuana when a knock came at the door. It was the hotel manager. Out went the joint, but the fragrance still hung in the air as he walked in, his nose twitching.

'Ah, you smoking hashish, no?' I thought the game was up, and I was expecting a repeat of my drug bust in Kenya, but instead, he turned out to be a nice guy who despised the Ayatollah! He and his family resented the petty restrictions of Islamic rule, had no connection with the police, and seemed to appreciate what he saw as our act of defiance against the regime. We had a lucky escape.

Once I walked into what I thought was a restaurant, during Ramadan. I went in and looked over a low wall to see a pot of sheep's head bubbling away, and suddenly I didn't feel so peckish any more. Then a few sheepish faces with gravy stains around their mouths appeared around the corner; these were Muslims having a furtive feed and relieved that I wasn't the religious police making a raid.

By the time I reached Tehran, the dehydration I had suffered in Delhi had combined with the rigours of the journey to leave me sick, gaunt and in an emaciated condition. I was like a bag of bones. My fifteen-day visa at least meant that I could rest up for a while and consider my experiences.

Since I'd left Britain, this long trip had taken me to the Jewish state of Israel, the nominally secular country of India, which is the home of Hinduism, the Buddhist stronghold of Nepal, and now through two Islamic republics. It was impossible not to notice the difference that religion made in these places.

Here in Iran, the women walked around like nuns, their whole bodies swathed in acres of cloth. Repression hung in the air, and the people seemed cynical and hard faced, their attitudes cold and unpleasant. I put it down to the strict confines of their religion, but whatever it was it made me feel uncomfortable.

A bloke I met at a bus depot befriended me and confided how saddened he was that he was no longer free to live his life as he wished. Instead of the social life he had enjoyed under the Shah, now the most sociable thing he was able to do was sit and drink tea. He lamented that he had been one of the ones who had campaigned to depose the Shah, little realising how he would suffer under the new Islamic regime. 'If this is Islam, you can stick it!' I thought.

It was unfortunate that my chosen route should have taken me via Iran and Iraq while they were at war with each other. Perhaps it wasn't such a good idea to travel through a war zone—though we did manage to stay clear of any of the fighting and arrive safely at the border with Turkey. There were no bus routes into Turkey so I stood at the side of the road, levelled my thumb, and began to hitch.

Climbing aboard the first truck that pulled up, I was offered a friendly welcome and speedy transport through the beautiful countryside. I enjoyed the ride. The driver was good company, explaining that he was married with children. After we pulled over to the side of the road for the night, he produced food and booze for us to share, and explained that we would have to spend the night sleeping head-to-toe in the truck's cab.

Next day, I got him to drop me off at the first bus station to which we came, and I took a ride to Istanbul. An African bloke I met on the bus knew his way around the city. 'Follow me,' he said, taking me off to a guest house that he knew. It transpired that he was a merchant seaman who had jumped ship and was looking for another berth in Istanbul.

A few more coach rides and stopovers brought me into Munich, where I had arranged to meet up again with Leo. The bus was three hours late and Leo was not at our prearranged meeting point, but luckily he had left a message giving me a number to call. He picked me up straight away and we went around to his parents' house for lunch.

'You look like my husband did when he came home from the war!' his mum said, as she took in my haggard and run-down condition.

Suitably fattened up I stayed for a short while in Switzerland. This was followed by an abortive attempt to hitch into France. Eventually, I went back into Germany and Leo lent me the money for the train fare back to Britain. Sixteen months earlier I had set off for Sudan and Kenya— and ended up in India. It was good to see the lights of windy Romford again, and to taste my dad's home cooking.

6

Beneath Burning Skies

Back in drab old Britain, I was like a gramophone record stuck in the same old groove. The only important thing in my life was *me*, and particularly the problem of getting *me* back to Asia so that I could continue my travels. Nothing else mattered.

It was 1985, and market research seemed to be in vogue. I got myself a job as a door-to-door interviewer; they were crying out for people. For several months, a typical day's work would involve me in persuading bored housewives to try a new brand of baked beans, calling back a week later to see what they thought about it.

'Did you like the colour?' 'Were the beans the right size?' 'And how did they taste?' 'Oh, they tasted just like baked beans ... ?' As you can imagine, the work didn't really compare with my experiences in the mystic east. I was bored out of my skull most of the time.

High street interviewing, stopping passers-by to ask them questions, taxed my resources to the full. The questionnaire lasted about forty-five minutes, but I would kid unsuspecting members of the public that it would all be over in a few minutes. The secret was to keep them interested so that they wouldn't look at their watches and see that I was 'having them on'.

At least I didn't fill the questionnaires in myself, like some interviewers did. I helped it along, though, gathering general opinions in as short a time as possible, and then second guessing what their detailed responses would have been to the questions I hadn't had time to ask before they walked off.

Another job I tried was selling loft insulation, door-to-door. I started off well, but gradually the hyperbole and the lies I had to tell to sell the product and get my commission began to grate on me. It was a good product—I later bought some myself—but nothing could ever live up to the expectations which I built up in my customers. My sales manager loved it, but I gradually found it difficult to live with myself afterwards. I became more honest in my approach, but my sales figures plummeted.

I remember one customer in particular—a very lonely man whose only son lived in Australia. Reading between the lines of what he was saying, there had been no contact between them for some time, and he bought insulation from me simply as an excuse to keep me talking. I felt guilty for embroidering the truth with such a vulnerable person.

My boss couldn't understand why I suddenly became so hopeless at my job. I quit before I was sacked, looked at the money I had accumulated, and wondered where I could raise the rest of the cash I would need for a plane ticket.

Dad was pleased as punch to have my sister give him his second grandchild; but if he was looking at me to give him another, he was out of luck. For once I was celibate, and it was my sister's sex life that was causing concern. Sharon was now ensconced with her new husband-to-be, a chap whom we will call 'Doug', who was typical of the characters she had been dating. Doug was very different from her first husband, but their love for each other was real enough.

Living at home with my dad, I found time to write a story called *The Silicon Chip*, about a Russian take-over of Europe. It began with a scientist chap called Orme inventing a system for crime control. Criminals released into the community are inserted with a silicon chip; computers in certain homes are able to detect these chips and alert the police in the event of a break in. When the Russians take over, everyone has to be implanted with a chip which will cause their head to explode if they try to move out of the tightly controlled environment to which they are confined.

There was an underground Christian group in the story, and part of the plot sounds like something out of biblical prophecy, so I must clearly have been thinking about religion when I wrote it. I'm sure a psychologist could have a field day exploring what the story tells about the inner workings of my mind—and the aftermath of my 'Moonie' experience—but it's clear that I was expressing a resentment at being confined to one place, and a sense of alienation with the world, which seemed to want to mould me into an image and restrict me.

Travelling had become a means of escape. On the road, meeting new people and dealing with day-to-day necessities saved me from having to work anything through to a conclusion. I didn't need to make any commitments, and I could always move on if someone got too close to seeing the real me. Perhaps I was running from the pain of my mother's death, or the despair of being rejected by my natural parents, but I was probably just being selfish. I wanted everything my own way.

Eventually my dad took pity on me. He could see how desperately I wanted to get away from the doldrums of Britain again, so he agreed to finance my trip, on condition that I repaid him some day. I decided to go back to India and on through Thailand to Bali, though as usual my plans changed en route.

When I had visited the kibbutz in Israel, I had got to know a fellow traveller by the name of Paul Gilbert. A mutual friend discovered that Paul and I had independently booked on the same flight to India, so we got in touch and decided to travel together. Meeting at the airport departure lounge, we had so much news to catch up on, and so many new plans to describe to each other, we almost missed the plane. It's lucky that the flight was delayed or my third journey would literally never have got off the ground. Laughing, we ran down the connecting corridor into the jet, realising that we were going to get on like a proverbial house on fire!

The plane landed in the roasting Delhi heat, and we travelled—as swiftly as anyone can on the tortoise-like Indian transport system—overland down to bustling Agra. The Taj Mahal looked as beautiful as ever, every inscription vivid in the bright tropical sunshine. As in most Indian cities, cows wandered down the main street unheeded, and on the outskirts, no one batted an eyelid when buffalo herds were driven along the roadside. Yellow and black auto-rickshaws swarmed the streets like hives of wasps, their drivers ready to barter a price for each ride.

I spent a fortnight in Agra, waiting for my travelling companion to recover from a spot of 'Delhi belly', the colloquialism for the stomach upsets and diarrhoea which often beset travellers in India. Paul was surprised that I waited for him to recover, but I was in no hurry when we were getting on so well. There were no drugs involved, we just clicked with our sense of humour and we seemed to spend the whole day laughing at the same things.

Jaipur was our next stop, and then to Jaisalmer, out in the desert beneath a blinding sky. A lot of westerners were taking camel rides into the desert; but we just laughed at this exhibition of unadulterated tourism—we were too 'hip' for camel rides. Afterwards, we regretted our snobbery in not going!

Going down to Gujarat and back to Jaipur by steam train was a great experience. Paul had been given the addresses of local families by various friendly Asian shopkeepers in London, so we looked them up. They were very helpful and courteous, welcoming us warmly into their houses and making us feel at home. At last, I had the opportunity to see what goes on in a typical Asian home. We were show pieces, taken around to meet friends and relatives: 'Here are our English friends,' they would say of us, as though we were exhibits in a display case. It got up our noses a bit, but we were well looked after and it seemed a small price to pay.

At another village, the old man of the house showed us his fields. In one corner was a plain concrete shed, inhabited by a sick young woman, with half a dozen children at her feet. The poverty we saw contrasted with the relatively well-to-do people we had stayed with in Jaipur. 'She's anaemic,' the old man explained. 'She needs milk but she can't afford it; she's very poor, so she will die here,' he said matter-of-factly. We were stunned by the man's seemingly uncaring attitude, when he could easily have given her what she needed to save her life. His attitude spoke volumes to Paul and me. Paul was particularly shocked, though I had been partly hardened by my experiences in Africa. Together we cursed the class system which perpetuated such callous injustice.

The third family we stayed with in Gujarat were also wealthy; their claim to fame was that they were proud owners of a western-style toilet—most Indian lavatories are little more than holes in the floor. We were taken by these lovely people to see a famous Indian rock star in concert. I thought he was terrible, but the crowd loved him!

In Bombay—one of the most squalid cities on the planet—we stayed with a hospitable family of five. Though living in a tenement block, they were an affluent middle-class family with a servant and their own business. They pointed out a one bedroom flat opposite where twenty-two people lived; they thought the overcrowding was hilarious, but Paul and I weren't laughing. The family thought they were doing their bedraggled twelve-year-old servant girl a favour by employing her for a pittance. She worked all hours, and didn't even have a bed of her own—she slept on the kitchen floor.

Paul and I stayed a week, sleeping on the balcony. Once, we were whisked off to a posh wedding attended by many Asian film stars. We were amused that they all spoke English believing that it was beneath them to speak their native Hindi. The groom arrived on a white horse, and the spicy wedding banquet was delicious. But such ostentatious displays contrasted with the squalor and degradation which characterised much of Bombay.

From there, we took an overnight boat down to Goa—my intended destination on my previous trip. Now, two years later, I had finally arrived. It doesn't do to be in a hurry when you're on the road.

Once a Portuguese colony, Goa is the most westernised part of India, much favoured by hippies, drug addicts, and would-be seekers of enlightenment. The vegetation is tropical, with coconuts, peppers, ginger, betel nuts, rubber and bananas among the principal crops. Tea and coffee are grown too, at higher altitudes.

It was here that Paul and I started to fall out. I was much more laid back than he was, and my easy-going attitude began to clash with his forthright nature. I think he was going through a certain amount of culture shock, which somehow triggered a clash of personalities. The writing was on the wall as far as our travelling together was concerned.

We stayed at a Catholic hostel run by a friendly Irishman. The establishment was a refuge for European travellers who had become 'burnt out' by too much LSD abuse. We didn't quite fit, so one night was all we spent there. Even the workers seemed to walk around with glazed expressions, as though reliving the experiences of one too many acid trips. We sidled up to one bloke who seemed to be coherent, but after a few minutes' intelligent conversation, he 'flipped out' and began spouting gibberish. Paul and I looked at one another; this guy was three parts bonkers.

We were grateful to find more conventional accommodation for the next night, and, unperturbed by our experiences at the hostel, we soon scored some dope and joined in the hedonistic lifestyle. We discovered that some canny Indians ran tourist trips for Indian men to go and ogle European women sunning themselves naked on the beach. Goa is the only place in India where such open nudity is encountered.

Paul and I parted company there, leaving me to make the long overland train journey to Calcutta by myself. I fell in love with the place and ended up staying there for two months. I adored its ruggedness and its vibrancy, for which I could forgive its poverty and shabbiness. Its colours were dirty, but they reflected the real life that was lived on its hospitable streets. I made good friends quickly and visited many of the cultural spots.

In the guest house dormitory one night, a very pretty French girl asked one of the lads to massage her shoulders. He was making a pig's ear of the job, so I took over. 'I'm good at massage,' I said, and scarcely had I begun than she melted in my arms. When I'd finished, she was looking at me with her tongue hanging out and a certain look in her eye. You can probably guess what happened later that evening, when the lights went out. I was walking around with a cheesy grin on my face for several days afterwards.

I tried a dodgy black-market deal with some traveller's cheques which came unstuck; I spent longer than I had intended in Calcutta because of my need to replace the cheques. The British Consulate were sympathetic about my dire financial need, but they didn't really want to know, and offered no practical help.

I met a German traveller at the hostel who had lost his family in the allied bombing during the war. In his face, I saw something of myself; did I want to end up like him—a wanderer on the back of the world, with no place to call home?

My spirits lightened for a while when I met an Australian girl in Calcutta, called Sheila. She agreed to lend me some money, otherwise I would have had to join the hundreds of thousands of homeless people sleeping on the squalid streets. The bank authorities, to whom I had gone for replacement cheques, kept me hanging on for weeks before finally giving me the new ones.

While waiting, I started to smoke copious amounts of pot again; the local *bhang* shop became almost a second home. I popped down there occasionally for a choice of chemical 'highs' the way most people would go down to the off licence. Paradoxically, though dope was legal in Calcutta, alcohol was banned. Sheila had a serious heroin addiction, which I was soon in danger of sharing with her. We smoked 'brown sugar' together—unrefined heroin—for she had quickly introduced me to hard drugs.

Sheila eventually became my lover. We spent a night together talking; then one thing led to another. Soon the French girl was forgotten. She went off to Bangkok, to the further mirth of the other hostel residents. Sheila and I became inseparable. We visited several surrounding villages, and sat at the feet of a few friendly gurus—

who all seemed to be as stoned out of their heads as I was.

One woman we met said that she didn't like India. I loved the country, and when I asked her why she was there at all, she responded that she liked the meditation, but not the country. India attracts literally hundreds of thousands of visitors each year who are on some sort of spiritual pilgrimage. She was just one of the multitude searching for a guru, a true teacher to lead them safely to a spiritual destination—the home they have been seeking for many years which, did they but know it, they could probably find as easily in their own back yard.

I too was still searching, denying to myself every step of the way that my travels were really a spiritual quest to find the peace and security I knew must be waiting for me somewhere. Eventually Sheila and I parted; our desires to see the world, with our pre-booked tickets taking us to different countries, were greater than any potential our relationship may have possessed.

Bangladesh was intended to be my next stop. I was so out of my skull on dope that I left my passport behind in a locker at the Calcutta guest house where I'd been staying! After I'd gone back to collect it, I got a train as far as the border and noticed that, on the visa stamp in my passport, the words 'by air only' had been illegibly scribbled. The border guards looked to me for a bribe to let me through the land route, but I was so angry that I refused outright. I turned tail and went back.

It must seem as though I was staggering around the world in a narcotic haze, the international equivalent of a drunk staggering along the gutter wondering which bar to pop into next; but I had to remain clear-headed, and have my wits about me most of the time, in order to travel safely.

Thailand sounded promising, so an air ticket was

promptly purchased and I was on my way. Bangkok here I come!

I arrived in scorching Thailand feeling ill. Though I had felt nauseous during my last week in Calcutta, and had been unable to keep down my food, I thought I was just run down or dehydrated. At a friend's suggestion, I went along to a hospital where I took a blood test and received some bad news. I was very low in potassium, and urgently needed a course of treatment. I was given some tablets to take and went on my way, hoping that I hadn't contracted something worse. . . .

Since I had slept with a couple of prostitutes in Africa, I had developed a particular distaste for prostitution, but it was rampant throughout Bangkok. Some of the bars offered a variety of girls at various prices, dependent upon how attractive they were and how disgusting the tricks were that they were prepared to perform.

I began to feel sickened by it all. Someone had whispered in my ear about AIDS, which was just beginning to appear, so fear of contamination was a further reason I didn't go with any of the girls who came and sat on my lap at some of the clubs I occasionally visited. Eighty per cent of the men I spoke to who had had intercourse with the local whores had contracted a bad dose of syphilis or gonorrhoea, with a particularly high level of immunity to regular treatment. Many of the sad-eyed girls had been sold into prostitution by their impoverished families.

Several people in a hostel I was staying in in Bangkok (reputedly the sex capital of the world) told me of a beautiful Buddhist monastery in southern Thailand. It was highly recommended by everyone I spoke to, so I joined up with a Dutch chap who was going there and we caught a train down together. Standing at the railway station, the national anthem began to play over the public address system, and everyone stood still in respect. The dignity which the people gave to the country's anthem contrasted with the lack of dignity the country gave to its people.

Our destination was Chaiya, about nine degrees from the equator, located in the middle of a rainforest populated with snakes, scorpions, toads, frogs and lizards. The air was alive with the cawing of parrots, the chirping of crickets, exotic birdsong and a thousand other sounds that I couldn't place. Arriving at the austere monastery, we presented ourselves to the friendly abbot, asking to stay and study Buddhism. For a week I stayed in a primitive shed on bamboo stilts, with grass mats for bedding, before graduating to a hut of my own.

This dwelling hadn't been used for ages, so I was assigned the task of clearing a pathway around and under the hut—it, too, was on stilts—hacking back the undergrowth with an old machete, in the searing tropical heat. There were snakes everywhere, though they usually seemed more frightened of me. Each night, I was disturbed by the noise of large rodents running across the roof. One night, I popped out to relieve myself against a tree; turning, I saw an enormous brown and yellow snake coiled a few feet away, hissing at me!

'A day of silence, the first of ten,' I wrote in my diary, seated uncomfortably in the half lotus position at the commencement of a ten-day retreat which involved yoga, chanting, various meditations, and long periods alone inside the hut I had cleared. 'A million thoughts enter my mind, a myriad crazy visions which words cannot describe. I am to seek for wisdom and to discover the peace of my inner self being at one with nature. All I can say is that I feel a bit lost. Bad dreams come into my head and nonsense beats loudly in my brain, like ballroom rock 'n' roll.'

Theravada Buddhism is about losing oneself in order to

merge with the oneness of all being—at least that's the theory. The silence gave me a sense of calmness and tranquillity, though it was difficult to concentrate on nothingness without my thoughts drifting onto some trivial distraction, and I still felt a long way away from the Nirvana I had been told about. We had ninety minutes of yoga classes daily—including one exercise that involved standing on one's head!—which did little for me other than expose my poor physical condition: my bones creaked badly.

'Several hundred people sat prayerfully around the outer circle, each with incense, candle and flower in their hand,' I wrote about a ceremony the next day. 'After about thirty minutes, the monks began to chant and we walked slowly around thirteen times in a circle. My candle went out twice, and I got burnt accidentally by the candle of the old lady behind me.' I still don't know what the ceremony was all about. . . .

I fared better on day three: 'This afternoon, after posting a letter to Dad, I experienced briefly a strange peace of mind, like soft rain falling while the sun peak-a-booed from behind the clouds. Its rays gave me a vitality and an inner strength that showered through me reassuringly, like a warm breeze on a cool summer night.'

By day five, I was getting occasional glimpses of nature's subtle transformation into something slightly dream-like during my meditative breathing. I seemed to float past the trees, their browns, greens and oranges burning in my mind. I felt as though my mind and body were being pulled by some magnet-like energy, which certainly made a change from feeling the prickly heat that made me itch. With getting up before dawn cracked every day, I was getting tired, listless and irritable. The walk down the narrow forest pathway in the half-light of dawn needed to be taken very carefully, due to the many snakes that slithered across the path and disappeared into the undergrowth. I walked the path alone every morning, but soon decided that the snakes were more afraid of me than I was of them!

'Lose yourself and come to the nothingness that is Nirvana, giving out cosmic energy to the world,' exhorted the kindly abbot, the sound of monks chanting in the background, and statues of the lotused Buddha everywhere. It appealed to my thirst for New Age philosophies, and built up my sense of self-importance. On the other hand, when the monks gave their *dharma* talks, I felt they couldn't really relate to the basic aspects of everyday life, like physical attraction, desire and love.

Their spirituality was all about escaping from the world rather than transforming the world through the practical implementation of their beliefs. Strangely, I kept thinking of Jesus' example of how to live life to the full, and I spent most of day seven reading Matthew's Gospel.

There were two western monks at the monastery, from whom I was permitted to seek counsel during my retreat. I explained to one of them that I felt guilty that I hadn't cried when my mum died. I hadn't realised that Buddhism regards sin and guilt in a completely different way from the Christianity with which I had been brought up.

'There is no law that says you should cry,' said one of them. 'Everyone expresses grief differently.' This spoke volumes to me at the time, with the assurance that I shouldn't feel guilty.

Theravada Buddhism, like Hinduism, teaches a cycle of births and rebirths. We are all born countless times into countless bodies until we extinguish all desire; only then will we cease to be reborn, achieve self-realisation, and reach the state of nothingness which is Nirvana, the ultimate goal. Man is basically his own god, on his own in the universe trying to find his own way out. That sounded okay. I'll have a bit of that, I thought; yet there seemed to be no way in which I could make the ideas work for me. What was I to do?

'I've given up on the yoga lessons. I find myself with lack of inspiration, and the forest seems to be closing in on me from all sides,' I wrote near the end of the retreat. 'Early this morning we all went to the hot springs which I very much appreciated. Then I came back after breakfast and slept till 12.30pm. Oh well, the rest did me good! I didn't do much at all during the day; in fact I missed out on most of the meditations.'

The essence of Buddhism is contained in the eightfold path, I discovered. The eight steps on the path are right views, right resolve, right speech, right behaviour, right occupation, right effort, right contemplation and right meditation. I was getting all eight steps wrong! To follow Theravada Buddhism—unlike Mahayana Buddhism, a later development which is easier for the masses to follow—is virtually a full-time job.

I felt a right wally trying to practise all the exacting disciplines in my present confused state. My frustration and physical discomfort promised to give rise to anger at any moment. I wanted to scream.

The eightfold path towards self-realisation didn't seem to agree with my temperament; it gave me spiritual indigestion! The five precepts that Buddhists are expected to follow in daily living are: kill no living thing, even insects; do not steal; do not commit adultery; tell no lies; do not take drink or drugs. It was an understatement to say that following the Buddha was going to require extensive alteration to my lifestyle. Though I liked the emphasis on experiential faith, the meditation and the promise of arcane wisdom, I just couldn't get the hang of it all. Perhaps I would return here later in my trip, or maybe Buddhism itself wasn't really the spiritual home for which my soul was yearning.

My feet were getting itchy for the road again, so I took off to Ko Samui, a small island off the coast. It has now become a tourist trap, but then it was a stopping off place for travellers exploring the Thailand–Indonesia chain of islands. I lived in a hut enraptured by this tropical paradise island, living it up for two or three quid per day, recovering from the austerities of the monastery. My visa was only valid for two months, but I renewed it and later went back to its sunkissed shores for a second visit.

Believe it or not, you can actually get fed up with living on a paradise isle with nothing but a hut and a hammock. Even the palm trees, fresh food, beautiful girls and glorious sunshine got boring, and the golden sands began to lose their glitter after a few months. I needed to get on the road again, to gather some new experiences.

During my time in Thailand, I came to the conclusion that the country was generally a much fairer society than India. Buddhism, like Hinduism, is riddled with superstition, although not to the same extent. There was less poverty and oppression in Thailand; and nothing like the depth of sadness and resignation I found in India. In Thailand, I felt I had stepped into light, out of the darkness that was India, though others may have found it different.

Leaving Ko Samui, I went through Malaysia before following the advice of fellow travellers and trying my luck in Australia. From Georgetown, Penang, I flew to Perth.

7

Of Easy Virtue

Malaysia's hot, humid climate and colourful zest had already frizzled into a blur behind me as I settled into the airline seat on my flight bound for Perth. I'd been surprised at the variety of racial features I had encountered in Penang—oriental, Chinese and Indian faces, and a few European countenances—and many of these were represented in the plane seats around me. What a vibrant, multicoloured world I lived in!

I'd been astonished too at the variety of religious tradition I had encountered on my travels. It was not unusual to encounter a Buddhist in a Hindu country, or to chat to a Christian in a country which was supposed to be Islamic. People seemed to be the same the world over, each with their own cultural mindset, yet daily rubbing shoulders with people of other traditions and cultures. It made me realise how much of an island Britain is, culturally as well as geographically.

Adventure, escapism and a quest for new cultural experiences still drove me on as the balmy Australian coast came up in the cabin window, but the need to find myself, and to discover a way of expressing many of the pains and hurts I still felt bottled up inside me, were also coming to the fore as I considered my immediate future. I was grateful to have all these opportunities to see life in the raw—life with all its bewildering complexities and endless possibilities—and to see it for myself rather than vicariously through a television screen.

Each of the five billion faces on the planet seemed to have its own story to tell, and I wanted to hear them all. I wanted to experience everything there was to experience, and then to settle down to assimilate for myself what life was all about. Who was the person called Gordon Barley and where did he fit into the great expanse of the cosmos? What was life really about? Would I be able to get a cheap taxi at the airport to take me to a decent lodging house? What a muddle of thoughts and emotions tumbled around in my skull!

The only common denominator was my lack of commitment to anything and everything that I encountered.

It was the middle of the night when the plane touched down beneath the star-spangled Australian sky, so I 'crashed out' at the airport and caught a bus into Perth after the hot morning sun had risen. My first impression of the city—even from the bus—was that there were a lot of young women around. 'This is it! Nirvana!' I thought. 'With a sea of voluptuous women everywhere, I'm going to like it here.'

I had been given the address of a travellers' hostel in Perth, and quickly found the right part of the city, but stumbling around trying to find the correct street, the first three people I encountered all spoke with heavy Italian accents. I thought I'd come to the wrong country at first, but it transpired that this was the Italian quarter, and few people here could speak much English.

Perth has a population of close on a million, and it's the pearl of western Australia—a lightly populated state, where Greyhound buses are the most effective way of bridging the enormous distances. Perth is quite a way from the other major Australian cities. It has some of the best surf beaches in the world, and plenty of pubs and clubs to brighten the night life. Originally founded in 1829 as the Swan River Settlement, it was once a rough frontier town, but it's now not as tough as it's made out.

One of my first actions was to phone Melbourne, to renew contact with Sheila, the girl with whom I'd had an affair while in Calcutta. To my horror, I discovered that she had been at death's door with a serious dose of gonorrhoea. Her immune system must have been very low after months in India smoking unrefined heroin. She advised me to go to the nearest clinic for a check-up.

Somewhere along the line, had I picked up a serious dose of venereal disease, and passed it on? I suppose it would have been the inevitable and rightful consequence of the lifestyle I was leading, but it was humiliating all the same. A few years later and it would not have been Non Specific Urethritis I feared I'd contracted, but Acquired Immune Deficiency Syndrome instead. But I certainly didn't feel lucky at the time, as I waited anxiously for the tests and possible treatment for this sexually transmitted disease.

I phoned Sheila and assured her that I would never have slept with her had I known I might infect her, but she insisted it must have been me because she hadn't slept with anyone for ages before we met. So where did *I* get it?

It was certainly a relief to get the final test results and learn that I had the all clear. I would never take VD for granted again, or believe I would never catch a dose. I was celibate for several weeks after Sheila's warning. It felt good to be clean.

The Australian government had obligingly granted me a six-month transit visa. It didn't permit me to work in Australia legally, but that wasn't going to stop me. One of the first illegal jobs I did involved going down to Freemantle, and walking around with a sandwich board all day. 'Eat at Joe's' or something, I think the sandwich board said. It was some sort of sandwich bar, so I suppose this form of promotion was appropriate. . . .

A girl I met in a bar called me up a few days later, and invited me to stay with her for a few weeks while her father was away, and then I decided to hitch up to Carnarvon, several hundred miles up the roaring surf coast. The Great Western Highway looked more like one of the trunk roads that wind through east London, rather than the gateway to the great outdoors—but a truck soon pulled up and I was on my way into the parched Outback, home to all manner of snakes and dingoes. I've met some fascinating people in my hitching around the globe, but this driver bored the pants off me by talking about his 'exciting' hobby—bee keeping.

He dropped me off at a place on a map which was scarcely more than a glorified petrol station. 'Come over here, mate,' shouted a guy leaning against a fence. 'Where are you going? Come on, cobber, I'll give you a lift. I've just got to phone my wife first.' I climbed aboard his utility truck—a 'UT' in local jargon—with 'roo bars' on the front to fend off marauding kangaroos. The desert here looked very flat compared with the rolling dunes of the Sahara.

As we headed off into the pathless Outback, I was grateful to have got away from the bee-keeper and wondered what boring hobby my new driver was going to thrill me with. Train spotting, perhaps? In fact, George, as he introduced himself, transpired to be a very down-to-earth bloke. So earthy that the phone call he had made to his wife had in fact been to tell her he was picking me up, and to give her my description to pass on to the police in case I tried any 'funny-stuff' on the road!

We travelled the edge of a vast plain, sometimes the colour of dried blood, and sometimes tawny as a lion's skin, dotted with a few tall pale trees. The Australian bush is unique and haunting in its beauty.

Many of the species encountered here are rare, and some unique to this New World. There's the Tasmanian wolf, the emu, wombats and magpies, the fairy wren, koalas and kookaburras, locusts and duck-billed platypuses—not forgetting those furry things with big feet that hop about a lot! I laughed at some of the absurdities of Australian folklore, the jolly swagman camped by his billabong, the aborigine blowing his didgeridoo like a fog horn, and the absurd names—the echidna was often known as the 'spiny anteater', which sounded like something out of *Monty Python's Flying Circus*.

George took me into Dongra, intending to drop me off with a friend who had agreed to put me up for a night. The friend wasn't about and, in the end, George gave me a bed. 'Do you like cray fish?' he asked me. I nodded, not knowing what cray fish were! He pulled a couple out from under the cans of Fosters in his fridge—enormous great lobsters they were—and said, 'Here you are. You can have these for your tea.' They wouldn't have won any beauty contests, but they were quite tasty. I noticed that George seemed perpetually to be getting himself into arguments with people—usually over the size of fish that they'd caught. I think their 'pork pies' were bigger than any of their catches.

Soon I was on the road again, and I quickly hitched the rest of the way through the bush into Carnarvon. It was a small town, scarcely larger than a village, with plantations of tomatoes and bananas, and a thriving fishing industry. The snapper was the chief catch. A chap I'd met in the Perth hostel had told me there would be work here, but warned me that there would probably be no accommodation in the local hostel. I was lucky to be able to kip on someone's floor until a room came up.

We all got on very well together, hiring cycles and riding around the various plantations to try to find work, or lying about in the aromatic shade of a cool eucalyptus tree. I was attacked by three Alsatians at one plantation, and was left with bloody teeth-marks down my leg.

Eventually I landed a job and soon found myself in a conversation about spirituality with a gregarious Yugoslavian plantation owner. I wasn't the strong land worker he was hoping for, but I did my best with the back-breaking work in the sun, and the deep conversations about religion that he enjoyed.

Another time I went out as a deck hand on a fishing boat, trawling for snappers. I ended up with the unlikely combination of sea sickness and tennis elbow, and was dismissed from the crew without payment. 'Bloody pommie,' scowled the captain. 'You're not worth your keep, sport,' he told me. While I'd been at sea, I'd missed the chance of some easy money with a German film company who were crying out for extras. I felt sick as a parrot.

The easy-going atmosphere of this colourful backwater was relaxing, but soon the wanderlust came on me again. After a narrow escape from a bar room brawl, and a scuffle with some angry aborigines, I headed off on the road again, past the gum trees and southern beeches, like a latter-day Jack Kerouak.

The thick pound of the Indian Ocean and the skyscraper clouds to my right contrasted with the trackless desert to my left. Bob Geldof once shot a video out there, four hours drive from Perth, and described the weird scenery: 'Giant, phallic stumps of crumbling limestone point like stalagmites at the sky, and fossilised tree roots—relics of a heavily wooded primeval past—litter the valley floor. A fierce, hot wind blew all day.'

After a brief stay in Adelaide—spent in the typical middle-class Australian home of the parents of a girl I'd met travelling—I made my way to Sydney in New South Wales, the site of Captain Cook's original landing. The first penal colony was established nearby, with the first convicts arriving in 1788. When an official asked me if I had a criminal record, I said wittily, 'I didn't know you still needed one!'

'Sydney has an air of age and history about certain parts of it, which is quite missing from most Australian cities,' writes Tony Wheeler in the traveller's 'bible' *Australia—A Travel Survival Kit*. 'That doesn't stop Sydney from being a far brasher and outwardly more lively looking city than its younger rival, Melbourne.' Many areas of Sydney (population 3,200,000) are named after parts of London, such as Paddington and Kings Cross.

At the hostel there, I made some good friends with whom I'm still in touch today. Many of them now deny any shenanigans because they have since found important jobs—one of them as a barrister—but we all used to get completely smashed on drugs most weekends. I was a better cook than most of them; my lamb chops were a talking point for years afterwards when we held reunions back in London. 'You know where the shops are, and you know where the cooker is!' I used to tell them when they came around with their tongues hanging out. I'd only recently started eating meat again; I'd been vegetarian for most of my time in India and the Far East.

My first job in Sydney involved picking up rubbish at the cricket ground, before landing a 'cushy number' tending the gardens at a concrete factory. Rumours of a job going at a toy factory took me away from my gentle labour in the garden—in anticipation of earning a lot more money—but I got the sack after a few days! The other lads from the hostel fared about as well. One of my mates lasted just one day, and none of the others lasted much longer than a week. Furniture removing was my next occupation, but that didn't last long either. I pulled a muscle in my back and was off work for several weeks.

To get a free feed in Sydney, one had to suss out one's options. One of the better scams was to nip down to the local Hare Krishna temple, and queue up around the back where *prasad*—food that had been offered to the idols—was dished out at the end of the day. Along with many others—mainly European travellers—I was a regular customer for this 'free take-away'. One day, I got talking to one of the devotees who insisted that I earn my free grub by going down to the local park with him to feed the pigeons. I didn't fancy that, so I chose instead to work in the kitchen and to serve the needy people in the long queue.

I thought the Hare Krishnas' beliefs were very airy-fairy. I tentatively read the Bhagavad Gita and a few of the Upanishads. The Gita itself is quite easy to understand; but the five pages of commentary following each verse—which is supposed to explain the meaning—is totally incomprehensible!

My experiences in the Moonies had made me very cagey about a sect like the Hare Krishnas; I was only there for the free feed. Sects were less interesting than sex. I went to some of their worship evenings, but I was only showing willingness to learn about the cult in order to preserve my supply of free food. Cults are said to 'use' their members, but I had subverted this idea; I was using the cult to my own ends.

My next job saw me in top hat and tails standing outside a new night club inviting potential customers to look at the premises. I was expected to be the bouncer too, if anything went wrong, but everything ran smoothly and I was paid eight dollars an hour plus meals and drinks.

One evening the washing-up man turned up drunk and was sent home. I was asked to deputise for him, so I washed up after my day's work pulling in punters (and pulling the barmaids). The management were only going to pay me the washing-up rate, but I protested that I had helped them out of a sticky situation, so they relented and paid me my usual eight-dollar rate, making me the highest paid 'washer-upper' in Sydney!

Rather than pay me so much, they asked me, 'Why don't you sign on as unemployed, as well as working here?' I shook my head in disgust, taking the moral high ground. 'I'm not going to be a dole bludger!' I retorted indignantly. What a joke! They didn't know that I was working illegally, and that even my transit visa had expired two months earlier!

My next employment was with a charity that was intended to raise money for aborigines. I was working alongside an evangelical Christian, as it happened. It was a 'con' really, because only a small percentage of the funds raised actually went to the aborigine school for which they were intended.

My workmate, who claimed that God was calling me, took me along to his charismatic church on one occasion. I was put off by the antics of the preacher, who seemed an over-the-top caricature of an evangelical preacher. I was quite a screwed-up person at the time, and not really ready for all this tele-evangelist style preaching. My inner person was crying out for deeper meaning, but my feet were stuck firmly in the mire of the world—a woman on my arm and a pint in my hand.

My mates and I from the hostel dropped an 'acid' tab one evening and we went off into the heart of the city. Waiting for the powerful surge of LSD to take full effect, we came upon a group of Christians singing choruses in the open air. When I joined in and held hands with these Sydney Christians, I could feel a powerful buzz. These people had something which I didn't possess for myself—a deep peace.

Holding their hands seemed to send an electric shock through me. It niggled for a while, but I walked away quickly, and forgot them as the euphoria of the powerful hallucinogenic began to take over. Everything I saw and heard seemed transformed by the *impact* of the LSD.

We walked away down to the rocks near Sydney harbour, where the s o u n d of GUITAR MUSIC led us over to another group of ChRiStIaNs enjoying themselves in the w a r m evening air. '*Come on in and join us, brother!*' they shouted. This was getting 'spooky', as Dame Edna would say!

'No!' I called out, making silly g e s t u r e s and gently gently mocking them. I wasn't being nasty, it was more tongue-in-cheek dErIsIoN, and there was a compelling ATTRACTION about them from which I found it d i f f i c u l t t o b r e a k away.

In a nearby bar, my friends and I found ourselves in another s u r r e a l situation. We were talking with the HaPpY crowd sipping their drinks, but conversation was proving to be very difficult. It wasn't as bizarre as pint glasses turning into monsters, but something wasn't quite RIGHT.

Communicating with the other people in the bar was proving more difficult than it should have b e e n, even under the influence of the LSD.

'Do us a favour,' s a i d a v o i c e over my shoulder. 'Help me to get all these people back on the bus.' I turned in a SURREAL haze, half expecting to find Alice and the Mad Hatter standing b<e<h<i<n<d me, but this MAN seemed sensible enough, and explained to my great mirth that the people with whom I had had so much trouble c o m m u n i c a t i n g were all patients from a nearby psychiatric hospital, who had been allowed out for the evening!

My mates and I were NOT happy to oblige. Though

RELIEVED that it wasn't we who were having trouble communicating, the request freaked us out even more. Coming bAcK from the toilet, I found that I had become separated from my friends Rob and Stewart, and was wedgedinthemidstofthepatients being herded aboard the bus. I was CONVINCED that I would be taken off to the mental hospital with the patients. The LSD increased my paranoia, and I fought my way through the CROWD, finally grasping Rob and Stewart in a fond embrace. As we made oUr way back to the hostel, FACES looked ugly and contorted, and I was glad when the awful e f f e c t s of the drug eventually wore off.

That was the first and last time I ever took LSD.

Kings Cross was a very sordid area, which I came to know well during the five months I lived there. In the brothel next to the hostel where I stayed, were many girls of sixteen or seventeen who made it clear that they were available for a very reasonable rate. One girl who was mainlining on heroin explained that her parents had tried to take her away, but the local mafiosi had a powerful hold on the girls. I quickly became disgusted at the squalor of drug addiction which kept these girls enslaved to vice.

Why *do* men go with call girls? Is it because they are unable to develop normal relationships? Do they expect perversities from these girls that no woman would willingly perform without being paid? Or is it all a show of machismo, flaunting the social conventions of respectable society? I think all those reasons are valid, but often the main reason is the need for love. A prostitute has many talents—providing not merely sexual gratification, but company, a listening ear and an elementary counselling service. My heart went out to many of these despised prostitutes, so abused and mistreated, desperate for money to finance their drug addiction and kept in thrall by their evil pimps.

Eventually I tired of the seediness of Kings Cross and decided to head back to Thailand.

I was amazed at the changes that had taken place in the months I had been away from Ko Samui. The hut in which I had stayed on my earlier visit had been demolished to make way for more up-market accommodation. There were even plans for an airport to be built there, to turn the site into a massive tourist resort.

I was sitting in a little shack on the shimmering beach eating the wonderful fresh food when my New Zealand friend, Rob, whom I'd known in Sydney showed up. It was good to see him. We met up with a group from North London and considered travelling through Malaysia together. It was an idyllic life once more, with marijuana for breakfast, lunch and tea. The drug was sold under the counter in one of the restaurants.

I soon felt at home with the other groups of travellers for whom this Thai island was a Mecca, and commenced a short relationship with an attractive German girl. Unlike every other relationship I had been in until that time, I brought its demise upon myself by being too possessive. It was as though I had reached a point in my life when I required something more substantial than the cheap romance and romps which had been the hallmark of all my relationships up to this time. The girl had recently ended a long-term relationship and didn't want to become involved in another long tryst, so she discarded me in much the same way that I had been dropping sexual partners for several years. Now I'd been dropped like a hot brick, and it hurt.

Still, there were consolations. Sitting one day in a restaurant built on bamboo stilts, I watched the owner knock green coconuts off the nearby trees with which to make the most delicious—and freshest—pina colada I have ever tasted. The sky and the sea changed through myriad colours depending on the light and the time of day, but the sand remained white and soft.

This was perhaps as close as one could get to heaven on earth, I thought. The days were bright and filled with laughter, promising a thousand girls and a thousand thrills. (It didn't keep that promise.) The Thai massage relaxed me, and the bars stimulated me. There were videos to watch, games of Scrabble to play (honest!) and trips around the island to make, but after five or six weeks of this life I felt as though I had had my fill of the hedonist ambience. Unease hung in the air.

I felt confused and uneasy. It wasn't just the demise of the relationship that made me feel this way; it was as though the whole lifestyle had run its course for me. I needed to find a more permanent way of living that would allow me to be myself, but which would be more lasting, and more fruitful for my personal growth. I began to make definite plans to return to Britain.

The endless sleep, drugs and sex washed over me still, but emotionally I felt myself being stirred to make some change. I felt a bit unstable, and Paradise Island was becoming unsatisfying. I was free as a bird, but what did my freedom add up to? 'Freedom's just another word for nothing left to lose,' sang Kris Kristofferson. 'Freedom ain't worth nothing, but it's free.' That just about summed up the life I was leading.

We all went off to Penang, in Malaysia, with a view to catching a boat to Sumatra for a holiday from our holiday, but my unease still remained. Why was I so uncomfortable?

As it happened, there wasn't a boat for another two weeks, so we decided to go up into the stunning Cameroon highlands for a week or so. When we returned, and the night before our departure for Sumatra, I was chatting to two Dutch girls, back in Penang, when an Austrian guy I knew from the monastery came across.

'Gordon, can I have a word?' he said.

'How ya doing, mate?' I said uninterestedly. I didn't want him to invade my space, or to keep me from scoring with one of the Dutch girls.

'Gordon, I need to talk to you. It's about a telegram from your father,' he said.

'Yeah great, I got the telegram.' I'd written to my dad during my previous stay in Thailand, asking him to write back, and he'd sent a telegram by return. I'd been terrified in case it was bad news, but it had simply said, 'All's well, don't worry.' What a relief!

The Austrian guy still looked anxious. 'No, Gordon, I don't think you understand,' he said. 'Can I speak to you, please?' So I went off with this man whose face looked like it could curdle milk.

'Gordon,' he said, once we had found a quiet place. 'After you left the monastery, a second telegram arrived, bringing bad news. I'm sorry to be the bearer of ill tidings.' He took a deep breath and spat it out.

'Your father has died.'

8

The Edge of Insanity

I was a broken man. At last I truly understood everything that was meant by being totally 'gutted'.

I was completely knocked for six, though it was a blessing to be secure in the company of good friends, and one woman who had experienced similar bereavement was a great help. All the other travellers rallied around me in what felt like my darkest hour. By some miracle, I could remember an uncle's phone number, so I quickly called him up.

'Is it some kind of joke?' I asked hopefully.

'No,' he said solemnly. 'Your father has been buried these past four weeks.' His words broke up my world into tiny splinters. 'Your sister's moved into the house, lock stock and barrel,' he added bluntly. So not only had I lost the man who had adopted me and been the only dad I'd ever known, but it looked as though my sister was going to take over the house.

In a total daze, I smoked a cigarette and poured out my heart to my friends and travelling companions. In a numbed and surreal state I went off and bought a one-way ticket home. It would only have been another two weeks before I was scheduled to return anyway. I wasn't looking forward to going back. It was the longest and darkest journey of my life. The weight of the miles rested heavily upon me as I cast my mind back to the good times I had known with my dad; the half-formed plans I had made for the future; and the stories about my travels, which I had intended for my father, which would now never be told to him.

My father had been consumed by a nuclear holocaust and only the rapidly fading past, with its glossary of faces and incidents, remained for my comfort. I would have given everything to have had my father waiting on the doorstep for me, ready with a slap on the back and the kettle on the boil. But my hopes and dreams had been savagely violated. Why? Why? Why?

Wiped out and void of emotion, this was a homecoming to a home which no longer existed. I had no sanctuary to return to; the father I wanted there waiting for me was gone, and it seemed that my sister had set up a new home for herself in the embers. Desolation.

The wild parties I had known, the myriad women in whose ears I had whispered sweet nothings, and the balmy nights when the euphoric scent of a toke of marijuana had cradled me into sweet oblivion, now meant nothing to me as my jet liner touched down on the cold British tarmac. My grief was grey as ash, as deep as the grave, and nothing could console me. Bright highways were now forsaken tracks, starless and bible-black. Loneliness draped itself over my shoulders as I cleared customs and began the last leg of my longest journey. I felt empty.

Arriving back in Romford, I couldn't face going round to the old house, so I went instead to Dolly and George—old family friends whom I knew I could rely upon for comfort and support.

'We've got the front door key you left with us,' said Dolly. 'Your sister came around asking for it, but I told her that you'd left it in our care and I wouldn't let her have it; but she's obviously got a key from someone else, and got into your dad's house.'

They phoned up Paul, an old school friend, and we arranged to meet and go out for a drink. Paul had always been a slim lad, but sixteen stone of him walked through the door. 'I packed up smoking, and took up eating instead,' he said by way of explanation. I had to smile.

My breath misted in the late winter air as we reached the pub. My confidence bolstered by a couple of pints of Ruddles County in the popular seventies-kitsch bar, Paul and I went around to the familiar three-bedroom house, where Sharon had made herself at home. I'd hardly set foot in the door before I realised that everyone had misjudged the situation. She hadn't 'taken over' our dad's old house—in fact she found it spooky and could hardly pack her bags quick enough to get out. She had only moved in to prevent the place from being burgled.

There was Dad's old chair, and the garden he loved, with the fields beyond. There was the kitchen, where I could picture him standing by the chip pan. I went upstairs, threw myself on his bed and cried.

Later, I found a new suit that my dad had bought for himself, but which fitted me perfectly. How alike we had grown in the end!

Sharon had taken Dad's death badly, and I heard that some relatives had made unwarranted remarks about her at the funeral. Anger began to stir itself into the crazy mix of emotions I was feeling.

'Death is part of living, all creatures die,' I began to write, trying to get my thoughts into order—and failing. 'Why is it that so much pain and deep emotion is felt within Man? I can't begin to write about my sorrow. Maybe in time it will change, but now each day brings more troubles. Oh God, when will I see the end of it?

'Depression and pain are taking over my personality. I'm becoming moody and snappy with friends. The tension in my head, neck and right shoulder is crushing me. I need a release, like a passage to a better planet. For all the fun I'm getting out of life, I'd be better off being a monk—if I continue living.

'Strange things are happening to me. When I even begin to think that things can't get much worse, they do. I feel burned out. I say the wrong things. I know I'm not the only one with problems, but it still doesn't cushion the hurt inside me. I'm trying not to go crazy, but I feel that something evil is pushing me that way. Maybe prayer will help—and meditation. Abstaining from material stimulation could be a start, but a start to what?

'There are "answers" somewhere, but not in my sphere of understanding. Maybe if I was to attain the enlightenment of Nirvana . . .'

What a muddled, maudlin man I'd become!

Before I'd gone away, Dad had explained that he had made his will, but there was no such document to be found anywhere. We knew that he would have wanted my sister and me to share ownership of the house. We went to a solicitor for legal advice, then Sharon and I decided that I would buy out her share of the property. This house was my home—or the closest thing I had to one—and sentimentally I wanted to keep it. We agreed that the house was worth about fifty thousand pounds, so I decided to take out a mortgage, pay her twenty-five thousand pounds straight off, and then repay the mortgage over twenty odd years.

The family of Sharon's husband-to-be began whispering in her ear. 'Gordon's out to rip you off! Make sure that you get an independent evaluation of the property. It's worth more than he's letting on!' So she brought in an independent valuer by whose decision we agreed to abide. The valuer decided that the house was worth only forty-six thousand pounds, so the mistrust that had been planted in her like a poisoned seed had lost her two thousand quid.

Sharon and I got on fine dividing the furniture and the odd knick-knacks between us; it was her future husband's relatives who were trying to drive a wedge between us. I was worried about paying her the money, fearful that her in-laws would persuade her to fritter it all away. But what else could I do?

My solicitor was unhappy about handing over so much money; he too was suspicious about my sister's in-laws, but there was nothing legally that could be done. She was entitled to half the house. We were right as it happened—the in-laws took her for a ride, borrowing some of her money and not returning it.

When I went to enquire about a mortgage the woman behind the counter was hostile from the outset: 'You've been away for most of the last five years, and you have no job. Why should we give you a mortgage?'

'Well, I'm going to get a job, of course. My travelling days are now at an end,' I said, stating what was now obvious to me.

'There's no chance of us giving you a mortgage,' she replied. 'Even if you get a job for six months, there's no guarantee that you're going to keep it.' What was I going to do now? I had some cash that Dad had left me, so I wasn't in any immediate financial difficulty, but emotionally I was profoundly depressed.

My diary records my feelings at the time: 'They say that at times like this, people turn to religion, but religion confuses me more and more. Why is there so much suffering in the world if there is a loving God? It's so hard to pray when there is so much insanity going on, though I know I haven't tried very hard. I really need to understand more, or at least to think about it more. I know in the times before when I took an interest in religion, I ended up all the more confused.

'The company of a woman would be nice right now; it helps a man when he's lonely. I keep my fingers crossed that soon I'll be in the right place at the right time and say the right thing.

'It would be easy to run away—to start travelling again—but I've seen enough of other countries and had enough of making good friends that I never see again. I was looking forward to coming back to a home, with Dad pleased to see me again, and me glad to be home. My only worries would have been in getting a job and a few women. I don't know why my dad had to die so young. It hurts too much to think about it.'

Spirituality occasionally entered my head for long enough for me to decide to do something about it. I visited a spiritist church in Chelmsford where the medium claimed to have once cleared a whole house of spirits. 'They were very playful,' he said, but something about him made me feel uncomfortable.

Around this time, I also went to several Hare Krishna meetings held at the house of John Richardson, the ex-drummer from the seventies pop group The Rubettes, who now ran a reflexology practice. I met Hazel O'Connor there, too, chanting the Hare Krishna mantra with the others, though I felt unable to join in.

I found a job with a telex agency but it only lasted three months. Even this was got through dishonesty, as I fiddled the entrance test to make me look faster than I was.

I drifted into a series of part-time jobs—sometimes as a telex temp, but once as a park attendant—and I got myself a lodger to help make ends meet.

For years afterwards, I had a string of lodgers—some of whom were fine while others initially seemed to be very presentable, but later turned out to have run up catalogue debts for clothing, or were prepared to go off without paying bills.

The dawn of 1987 fell heavily upon my spirit. I had been home for a year, and the depression was not lifting. Friends rallied around me, but I found it very difficult to let people get close to me. I was frightened that I would lose people by clinging onto them too much. I had only one brief sexual relationship in all that time; and she left me because of my possessiveness with her, in what was really only a squalid casual affair.

I had let down my defences and allowed this girl into my life; but I was so besotted with her that I didn't see the squalid sex sessions for what they were—expressions of lust and not of love.

I decided to get out of the country again for a short while, so booked a return flight to Spain. Torremolinos was like a tacky version of Blackpool, so I quickly regretted my decision. With my bit of Spanish, I soon found myself a room; but there was little in the place that looked likely to raise my spirits.

I wandered into a small coffee bar and—would you believe it—the place was run by Christians. 'Could things get worse?' I thought. Still, I fell into conversation with the lady behind the counter.

'Have you got one of these?' she asked, offering me a Gideon's New Testament. I had, as it happens, always taken a New Testament with me on my travels, and read it from time to time—as I had done in the Thai Buddhist monastery. But as I was only in Spain for two weeks, I had left it back in Romford on this occasion. I gratefully took the copy she offered me.

'Are you here for long?' she asked.

'Only till the morning, then I'm off to Granada.' I couldn't wait to get out of the place!

'Why don't you visit our farm?' she suggested. It seemed that the Christian group to which she belonged ran a farm which operated as a rehabilitation centre for people with drug problems and emotional difficulties. 'I'll go for that,' I thought, hoping that this wasn't going to turn out like the 'Moonies'.

The farm took some time to find; it was several miles from the nearest station, in a dry, barren countryside. The man who ran the place was out in the fields, milking the cows. I went out to see him. It turned out that his name was Gordon, too.

'Ah, ma wee lad,' he began—he really was an archetypal Scotsman. 'Are ye a Christian?'

'Yes,' I lied straight-faced.

'Gud laddie. Sae, wit kirk d'ye gae tae?'

What church do I attend? You must be joking!

'Oh, I don't believe you have to go to church to be a Christian,' I affirmed.

'Is 'art reet? Ye nae 'av' tae gae tae kirk?' he shook his head. 'A *Christian*, eh?'

The young people on the farm were from all over the world, though mostly from Spain. It was mainly a dairy farm, though there were a few crops growing in the dusty soil. They let me stay the night, and a few of them shared their faith with me, emphasising my own sinfulness and my need of a saviour, but I didn't want to know.

The following day, I made my way to the town of Granada, where I wound up sharing a room with a German medical student. He met an English girl the next day but, since he had a girl back in Malaga, I ended up 'hitting it off' with her. She and I spent the next ten days or so travelling around Spain and Morocco, drinking copious amounts of Tequila some nights, and enjoying the Spanish cultural experience.

Morocco was beautiful. Its rolling hills and valleys were

all shades of green, yellow and brown; but I found the people unattractive. That was probably more a reflection of my own depressed state of mind.

'In a bar in southern Spain, I sit waiting for inspiration, while mid-morning chatter goes on and sweet sickly cigarette smoke fills the air,' I wrote one languid day. 'I'm drinking beer while the locals drink coffee and cognac. It's raining in Spain and there's not much to be enthusiastic about, but life rolls on regardless.'

I felt as though I had a big black cloud hanging over me, and a black dog tearing at the seat of my trousers. I could almost taste my depression and it showed no sign of lifting.

Returning to Britain, I smoked my way through a big stash of hash and pondered my life. Sex and drugs were no help to me. As Neil Young sang, 'Every junkie's like a setting sun,' and the daylight was certainly fading out on me. Travelling simply took me round and around in circles. I'd lived the kind of carefree lifestyle that many men my age would have envied, but the scores of women and the dozens of drugged stupors had taken me precisely nowhere. What did it all mean? Not a sausage! There was no place where my heavy load could find solace and rest. 'I have run too far, and swum out of my depth too often. I have sung songs with no meaning and spoken empty words,' I scrawled in my self-pity. I think it was the drugs talking again. 'The pain of reality crushes some, and merely scathes others. Some play around with fire of emotion, and others have been burned and disfigured.

'I am guilty and innocent, confused and enlightened, afraid and comforted because I am human. Because I, in my darkest corner, seek God. I seek ultimate truth. I cannot *keep* running. I cannot *keep* falling. I am not a stranger in a strange land, as I have been. I know my heart's desire, and that desire is for good!'

Where was God hiding? What powerful spiritual searchlight could seek him out? Buddhist meditation had bored the socks off me. Hinduism seemed steeped in superstition. Islam was far too puritanical for my taste. And Christianity was . . . well, it was. . . .

I paused for a moment.

Actually, the dozens of Christians I had met, and who had befriended me all over the world, had seemed very down-to-earth individuals. The only remotely outlandish thing they had to say was that God, who made the heavens and earth, deeply cared for people like me. Well, who would credit it?

What the heck. What did I have to lose? Perhaps the time had really come to stop running. If it was true what those Christians in Spain, Australia, India, Israel, Greece, Zaire and back home in Britain had been telling me—and considering that none of them knew one another, they all told a pretty consistent story—then perhaps I ought to give the Christian God a chance.

At about that time, an old friend and near neighbour, John Levick, asked me to be the best man at his wedding. I suppose he thought that my gregariousness would guarantee a good speech. In fact, I made a cack-handed botch of it, but the wedding led to renewed contact with Derek and Barbara Levick, whose Sunday school I had attended as a young lad.

The church John's new in-laws attended was quite lively, or so I'd heard—plenty of hand-clapping and arm waving. This intrigued me and appealed to the hunger and thirst I held in my soul for some sort of truth and reality in a form that was culturally relevant to my own life and experience. Perhaps this Romford Community Church might provide some direction to my quest for a spiritual home where my heart could find some ease, before that long-expected nervous breakdown caught up with me. I thought I might go along there one Sunday.

At the wedding, Derek sat down next to me and asked me, 'If you were a minister at a church, would you prepare your first sermon, or would you "wing it" relying on God's inspiration?' What an odd question, I thought.

'I'd probably rely on God the first time, then prepare the next sermon,' I answered. Where was this leading? I'd had a few drinks and I was shaking with mirth, so I don't remember how the conversation proceeded, but it was to prove strangely prophetic. . . .

The Romford Community Church was a charismatic offshoot of a traditional Baptist church. It was very lively when it needed to be, but solemn in all the right places. It met for worship in an infant's school hall, in Gidea Park, Essex. The area has always been quite middle class, and the congregation, as a whole, reflected the local population. They welcomed me with open arms, and I immediately felt accepted. I started attending one of the home groups, too. Soon I was going fairly regularly, and thinking about looking at the Brentwood Road Evangelical Church, just to see what were the differences.

A little later, I decided to visit the parents of my old mate Trevor Bacon, who happened to be living temporarily in the manse (the minister's house) of the Brentwood Road church. I thought I might be able to find out a bit more about the church before I visited one of its services. Trevor's sister Penny was there and we got chatting. She invited me back for coffee with her and her husband, Bob, a professional musician who had worked with some big names in the music business.

Sitting in the front room of their home, I told the story of my travels, describing the many religious faiths I had encountered along the way. Bob and Penny Cranham were startled by how much Christian jargon I had acquired through my interactions with different believers. They were surprised that I had never made a full commitment to Christ, in spite of encountering so many believers—and despite my sincere beliefs both that God exists and that Christ is his Son.

'Do you believe that Jesus is the only way to reach God? That he is the Way, the Truth and the Life?' they asked.

'Yeah, sure,' I said. I had no doubts on that score. Though still 'hung over' from the different spiritual influences to which I had recklessly exposed myself, I was prepared to accept that Christ is the only way to God.

I explained that I felt very guilty about many of the actions I had committed in my life. The way I had abused most of the relationships I had ever been in now filled me with deep shame. I asked God to forgive me for all the hurtful things I had ever done to other people—and particularly for the way I must have hurt God himself. As Bob and Penny spoke about Jesus, his desire to forgive those who don't try to conceal their wrongdoing, and his willingness to strengthen those who call for his forgiveness, I felt a deep tranquillity.

'Do you feel a sense of peace?' asked Bob. 'Do you feel the Lord here?' It was as if he could read my mind.

'Yeah! I've not felt this good since before my father died.' I couldn't stop smiling! I was sitting there grinning like a Cheshire cat as we spoke of God.

I was curious about what one had to *do* to become a Christian. Was there some special ceremony, or a special form of words that you had to say? Did you have to have a priest to say some special words? Was there something I had to sign? Was this something I could only do in a church?

As we talked on into the night, I said that I would like Jesus to be a real part of my life. I even said a prayer to that effect, right there in the Cranhams' front room. I didn't want to become 'religious' or a 'Holy Joe', but if Jesus could accept me as I was, and help me to stop taking drugs and screwing around—to give me the strength not to do the things which were driving me to despair—then I wanted him in my life.

'How can I become a follower of Christ?' I asked, sincerely committed to making this step of commitment, no matter what it involved, or whatever the cost. 'When can I become a Christian?'

Bob and Penny Cranham smiled warmly.

'You just have . . . !'

PART THREE

Getting a Life

9

A Window on Eternity

I had acknowledged God's sovereignty, accepted my own sinfulness, asked to be forgiven, and pledged myself to follow Christ. That was all it took to make a new start. It was that simple!

He'd been knocking at my door for years, so what made me say 'Yes' to Christ in the end? I think if I hadn't accepted him there and then, I would have been in for a nervous breakdown. I knew I couldn't handle the growing depression.

The night before, I had met a sexy girl in a nightclub and had made arrangements to meet her. This was potentially a return to a very familiar lifestyle. Was this something I would need to give up to be a Christian? The prospect worried me, but if this was the sacrifice I would need to make—to refrain from these short promiscuous relationships until the right girl came along for me to marry—then so be it. I never did meet that girl again.

To keep me away from temptation—and to learn about the Christian faith I had just embraced—I arranged (through the Cranhams) to spend several weeks at Pilgrim's Hall, a Christian conference centre out in Brentwood, Essex. For three months I lived there, working as an odd job man, and receiving Bible teaching and counselling. It is a lovely country house set in acres of beautiful countryside. I came to love the place dearly, and it was a real home-from-home through the autumn of 1987. I was grateful to Bob and Penny for introducing me to such a restful place with a warm and friendly atmosphere.

I was able to continue paying my mortgage out of the savings that I had accumulated—and from the remains of the money which my dad had left me. People told me to lie about my savings and to get my mortgage paid by the DSS. It would have been a poor start to a discipleship course to have done so.

I received prayer and deliverance from all the lifestyle disorders that I had acquired during my travels. I was fully in control during these 'deliverance' sessions, and didn't pass out in the way some do. I was having the spiritual 'gunk' of my past promiscuity and quasi-religious dabbling prayerfully drained from me.

Peter Garrett and Doug Day were a great help to me as I fought to dispel the last vestiges of the big black cloud that had followed me around like an enormous weight, threatening to crush me at any moment. Soon the light was shining through the darkness and dissipating the ugly depression that I had thought would never leave. I laughed and cried in that house, spending my days cutting up trees that had been blown down in the winter storms, tending the grounds, sweeping up the rusty autumn leaves as though they were the crinkled scales that had fallen from my eyes, and generally finding my way about in the new faith that I had embraced.

At Pilgrim's Hall, I sorted out the many dodgy spiritual practices and beliefs which I had accumulated from the smorgasbord of world faiths during my travels. I was not strictly vegetarian at that time, because I also ate fish, though the lamb chops were now a thing of the past; but

I had become a 'faddy' eater, seeing merit in eating certain foods, when no such merit really existed. Gradually my eating habits became more conventional.

I had believed God to be present in nature to an extent that was incompatible with Christian theology; not simply viewing the world as his creation, but subscribing to the New Age view where God can be seen as *a part of* all of creation—instead of *apart from* it. I thought that God was energy and that he was in everything. I'd been so steeped in pantheism that even a brick was a living thing to me—and filled with God, to boot!

I had to be taught that God is a designer—separate from his designs, but sustaining them in existence by his creative power. I was in need of spiritual food, and 'knowing the *creation*' was not enough—exploring the planet, living in harmony with the world, or not eating meat, would not suffice—I needed to know more of the creator God. I was glad to have Peter and Doug there as my teachers. Chris Hill, who later became Principal of London Bible College before returning to itinerant ministry, taught me from the Bible.

It was exciting to get to grips with the astonishing theology of John's Gospel. St John did not see the events of Jesus' life simply as events in time. He saw them as windows looking into eternity. The miracles were more than one-off supernatural events; they were Technicolor pictures of the reality which Jesus always was and is! We will never fully comprehend the ultimate mystery of God in this life but God the Father—forgiving and all loving—has become incarnate in the historic person of Jesus Christ.

All through the Old Testament, I learned, people had warred with God, and those who were faithful to the creator were few and far between. But still, through signs and miracles, testings and much pain, God made himself known through the words and deeds of often eccentric and maligned prophets. Until Jesus came, though, God was not fully understood or loved—only feared for the most part. Jesus made God known for the first time as infinitely compassionate and loving.

'Jesus Christ is our doorway to God's truth, from darkness to light, from illusion to ultimate reality,' I wrote in my notebook. In him, all the messianic prophecies of the Old Testament have their culmination. He bore all the sins and wickedness of the world on his broad shoulders when he was nailed to the ugly wooden cross at Calvary. At this point, when Jesus was hanging naked upon the cross—and all the transgressions of mankind were heaped upon him— God the Father turned away from the wickedness that Jesus had come to represent. God tore apart his own essential being as the price of his own righteous judgement. The grace he bestows is not cheap; it required God to divide his essential divinity, and for a part of that divinity to taste death!

Since the fall of our first human parents, God—though tempted to destroy the world and end our sinfulness—*kept on loving us*. All through the ages the good Lord was trying to show us the way back to him, to open the doors of our heavenly home and welcome us in. But through our ignorance we were constantly unfaithful, even worshipping idols of our own creation. His Final Solution was not genocide but deocide, the physical death of God fully incarnate, the one in whom dwelt the complete being and majesty of the supreme God, full of grace and truth.

'Humiliate me! Spit on me! I'm still your loving Father. I'll never turn you away. This is how much I love you! Now will you love me back?' This is our God. This is our heavenly Father.

Christ gladly bore all my own debauchery and lustful passions, the self-abuse I committed with my drug-taking, every wrong word I ever spoke and every wicked deed I ever committed. He carried them all within his own perfect being, in order that the price of my sins could be paid with his sufferings, and I could truly go free. This was a greater love than I had ever known, greater than the world has ever known: a love that knows no limit or measure. As Charles Wesley wrote:

> Were the whole realm of nature mine,
> That were an offering far too small;
> Love so amazing, so divine,
> Demands my soul, my life, my all.

The Lord Jesus came back to us after his resurrection. Even though his followers had denied him and ignored him when he needed them the most, his first words to them were 'Peace be with you.' And after his ascension he sent the Holy Spirit to empower his followers. His death wedged open the door to reality and eternity, through which we can all go home to God, simply by accepting Christ's free gift and returning his unconditional love with our own. How amazing is the grace of God, whose boundless love and wisdom were fully manifest in Jesus Christ!

Here, at last, was a framework large enough to encompass all my spiritual desires and yearnings. It was the map for which I had sought in my wanderings across the globe! On this chart, shown only here, was a place marked which I could recognise as the culmination of everything my feelings about a proper home had come to mean to me. It was where I truly belonged!

Here was no sense of oppression, or countless rules to follow, or strange esoteric ideas to embrace. *Here was a person to love, not a set of regulations to follow*. I felt that I knew who I really was at last. Coming to Christ was like a glorious homecoming—yet it was no sudden arriv*al* but rather a continuous arriv*ing*. I will not finally be with God till I die, and go to meet him in his glory. But I know that *I shall be with him one day*, and stay with him for ever in the place that he has prepared for me, because—in the Cranhams' living room—I made the essential step, took the ticket Christ paid for me to have, and finally 'got on the bus'—after years of letting so many earlier buses pass me by!

After my three world treks, I was now commencing a new adventure—the journey of my immortal soul through a far country to a destination where my arrival and welcome are well assured. This journey will take me along routes stranger than any ever encountered in the rainforests of Africa; under the fiery skies of India; on the vast Himalayas; within the vice dens of Thailand; or inside my wildest dreams!

I had been far away from my heavenly 'dad', and there were many hurts I had suffered which could not be healed overnight. The process continued at local church level, as I began to integrate myself back into the church community. At the Romford Community Church, I completed a five-week commitment course, one evening a week, with other new Christians. Here we discussed and learned more of what this 'church-going lark' was all about. I joined a weekly home group where members met to study the Bible over a cup of coffee. In spite of being unashamedly working class I was never made to feel like their poorer cousin but was always welcomed into their homes.

The fellowship gave me a wonderful grounding in my new faith—through the examples of others' security and their knowledge of the love of God. Those early days did not pass without mishap, mistakes and struggles, but these kind people were always there at the end of a phone.

Despite their maturity, love and dependability, I soon couldn't help feeling that the church needed to get out of its huddle and into the community! At that time (mid-1989) there were discussions about how the church might be more relevant in reaching out to local people. A counselling service was planned, by committed church members who were qualified nurses, for pregnant women who were seeking a termination; but this step in the right direction sadly came to nothing. No church is perfect, and water-walking is a skill still to be learned!

When I returned to my Romford home that fitted me like an old shoe, I first found a job with an engineering firm in Brentwood and then had another stint as a park attendant. At the engineering firm, where I over-zealously wandered about singing gospel songs, I worked with a chap called Wally, a middle-aged man whom I began to evangelise. I was ill-prepared for this; it was all too sudden, but I didn't realise that at the time.

'Do you want to know Jesus as your Lord?' I asked him after a few weeks of preparatory conversation.

'Yes, I do,' he replied. I was overjoyed. Wally said a simple prayer and invited Christ into his life, as I had done. Afterwards, his workmates gave him a very hard time.

'How's Jesus then? 'Ow yer getting on wiv God?' they would rib him as he queued up for his tea in the works canteen. Wally couldn't take the ridicule. Mentally, he was a slow learner and a little unbalanced to begin with, and he quickly developed signs of neurosis and paranoia. He became convinced that every driver who came to the factory with a delivery was 'out to get him'. Poor Wally ended up having a nervous breakdown.

By this time, my sister Sharon had been taken into a psychiatric hospital again. Once, when I went to pay my weekly visit, I found Wally there as a patient. In leading him to Christ I had actually been undermining his grip on reality. He probably hadn't really understood the awesome significance of encountering the living God. His 'conversion' had perhaps been done simply to please me, or as an escape route from deeper problems. My ill-considered evangelism had possibly done him more harm than good. I was devastated. I realised that I was going to need proper training and guidance before I could share my new-found faith effectively with others. Also, I was experiencing opposition in my new life, in spite of my sincere desire to make progress and to share with others the treasure that I had found.

There were some people around me who blamed me for my father's death, considering that he had pined with worry about me when I was away on my endless travels. That would have been a heavy burden to bear had it been true, but in my heart I knew that my dad was very proud of me for travelling the world on my own, and returning with entertaining tales of exotic places.

Dad had been proud of the occasional 'traveller's tales' that I sent home, and which were published in the local newspaper. He had told me as much just before I had left on that final trip. The accusations caused me a little stress, but nothing was going to lure me back into a guilt trap. I knew that Dad had lived a good social life with his closest friend, Joan. He was certainly no lonely and embittered man, fretting about his son.

At Sharon's wedding, she told me that she had to go back to Warley psychiatric hospital. 'What shall I do, Gord?' she pleaded with me. I was stunned. Bumming a cigarette, I had gone outside for a think, when Sharon's new mother-in-law came up to me and suggested that I had contributed to my father's death by adding stress and worry to his life, by travelling as I did. It was hard to have this subject brought up again at a moment when I was consumed with anxiety about my sister.

While I was outside, wracked with emotional pain, a van

pulled up and out jumped an old friend from my Boys' Brigade days. Kevin Bell was a strong Christian, working with British Youth for Christ. 'I was driving down the other side of the main road when I saw you, Gordon,' he explained. 'I turned around to come and see you.'

'You've been sent by God,' I replied, and I explained the double blow I had just received. He prayed with me on the spot.

New Christians often seem to feel enormous pressure from the devil in their first year or so of Christian commitment, and I was no exception. I was about to go back to Israel for a holiday when I found certain tensions with a local Christian leader. 'Is that how much you love your sister? She's mentally ill and you're just going to leave her, are you? Is that how much you care?' It was the old guilt trap in a different guise. My sister was glad for me to take a break, so what business was it of anyone else's?

The pastor of one local church to which I was considering moving my membership, seemed to be constantly challenging me with an abrasive and abrupt attitude. He seemed as unfeeling as a stone wall. I was not actually a member of his church, and I did not recognise him as having spiritual authority over me at that point. I wondered at first whether the real problem lay in me having some sort of stubborn spiritual pride which prevented me from submitting to him. I later discovered that others previously in the congregation had also experienced him aggressively trying to dominate them and to run their lives. I resolved that he wasn't going to dominate me!

His attitude was simply not biblical. The Bible shows that pastors are meant to be like loving shepherds—the servants of the flock—not aggressive manipulators of people's emotions. He was well out of order.

I tried to keep the balance right, between becoming so 'humble' that I would really be nothing more than a doormat for people to walk all over, and being spiritually arrogant. This was all part of growing in the faith.

When I arrived in Tel Aviv, I was soon sitting in a bar minding my own business when a woman came up and said, in quite lurid terms and with strong innuendoes, how much she fancied me. Another temptation, but one to which I didn't succumb. At the end of the holiday, I managed to miss my charter flight; I'd got the day wrong. In all my travels, I'd never done *that* before!

Perhaps God was behind it because as a result of missing the plane, I met a British guy who explained to me how disillusioned he had become with Christianity—and how he was seeking to become Jewish! He was even planning to study Hebrew. In response, I gave him a book written by a Jewish Christian, which perhaps made him reconsider what he was doing.

Back at home again, I felt very vulnerable for a little while, and it was at that point that I made a serious slip back into my old lifestyle. The devil knew where I was weakest, and he hit me below the belt.

My previous inability to keep my trousers on when alone with a pretty girl came seriously to the fore again, when a holiday romance got out of hand. I ended up repenting on the bedroom floor for hours afterwards. The old idol of lust had crept back into my life, and would return twice more before I was able to smash it for good.

Shortly afterwards, an old girlfriend phoned me up and told me that her marriage was over and that it was me she really loved. She pleaded with me to see her, and vivid memories of our fiery, passionate relationship tempted me. But I knew better this time.

Just as Peter denied his Lord three times, so I denied Christ three times—each time just long enough to fornicate. Each time, I turned in shame and asked for strength not to do it again. Like Peter I was forgiven, restored and strengthened until I felt my self-control take command of my passion.

How was I going to stop these problems from constantly tripping me up? I began to think seriously that full-time Christian work was the answer. I needed to be concentrating on the Lord all my working day if I was not to be caught out by Satan. Some kind of social work might do the job, perhaps abroad, but more likely in Britain. I considered one job in southern India, but it would have been too easy to slip back into my licentious travelling lifestyle. Besides, I wanted to stay with my cultural roots. Somewhere in East London would be my best bet, I concluded.

Talking with friends about the sort of job I wanted, someone suggested that I try doing evangelism with an organisation called Mustard Seed.

For a few days, I was part of a team assigned to a small church in Hackney, with a Baptist minister named Steve Latham. We were paired off and selected some local tower blocks on the Nightingale Estate—wet beneath the gun metal urban skies—overlooking Hackney Downs, for door-to-door visitation. The whole decrepit estate looked like a film set for some grim science fiction epic, set in the future when society has broken down, and people live barricaded in the crumbling ruins of leviathan buildings like the skeletons of ancient giants. I was grateful to be paired off with Mary, a very mature middle-class Christian lady. We were like chalk and cheese, but we complemented each other well.

One woman let us come in to talk. As we entered we spotted bits of occult paraphernalia here and there; some witchcraft books, tarot cards and the like. They had become fetishes or talismans to her. They were oppressing her, but she was afraid to get rid of them for fear of some occult backlash. After a long conversation, we left and I returned shortly afterwards with Steve Latham. We took away two carrier bags of these occult trappings, and burned the lot in Steve's back garden. The woman gradually began to come along to Steve's church.

I had purchased an African necklace during my travels. Years later, I discovered to my horror that it was actually an occult fetish! It comprised a mammal's head, a big nut, and other bits and pieces on a bit of string. I soon got rid of that once I discovered its true nature.

Another young woman let us in, explaining that she didn't usually open the door to anyone. 'I usually let the dog bark to scare visitors away.' It seemed that she had been thinking a lot about God lately and was glad to have someone to explain Christ's message of good news to her, and to pray with her.

Every time we went out, something amazing happened to us. There was a friendly black geezer who was reading books from the Mormons and the Jehovah's Witnesses. We were able to put him on the right lines, with a healthy dose of Scripture!

At one flat, the door was opened by a transsexual man, who went by a woman's name. I think he was trying to shock us. He too had been contacted by the Jehovah's Witnesses but he felt very *judged* by them. 'I don't feel judged by you,' he said reassuringly. Steve Latham made several follow-up visits, and the last I heard the man had stopped cross-dressing, seemed a lot happier, and had started calling himself by his proper name instead of a woman's name.

An elderly Muslim couple invited us in for a fascinating conversation about the common roots of Christianity, Judaism and Islam. We noticed that the wife had a badly swollen foot, and Mary prayed for her disability. Next day, they phoned up the church to say that a lot of the pain had gone, and could we go back to pray some more!

I learned two lessons from these experiences. First, it was only by going out in God's strength that the doors opened to us. If we hadn't prayed, I'm sure that we would never have got inside any of these fortress-like dwellings. Secondly, though I enjoyed sharing my faith in this way, I also wanted to be able to stay in touch with the people I met. I desperately wanted to be rooted in a community rather than being an itinerant worker. I was sick of all the constant change.

On the second placement as part of the practical Mustard Seed evangelism experience, I was based in Highbury and Islington, working alongside an elderly nun named Sister Agnes. She used to bound up to tough looking youths and forcefully confront them with the gospel. It was extraordinary watching the way these burly louts melted in her smile, and warmed to her as though she was their long-lost grandmother!

'Jesus loves you so much,' she would say gently. The Billy Graham Mission '89 was happening in West Ham at that time, and we persuaded many people to go along and give the great American evangelist a fair hearing.

This led on to a period working with Terry Diggins of Plaistow Christian Fellowship, in the London Borough of Newham. Geographically it felt a good place to be. But doing what? Then I came across details of a job available at the Mayflower Family Centre in Canning Town, not far from Plaistow. They wanted a community worker and I reckoned that I might just fit the bill. I sent off my application and was called for interview.

Canning Town is a tough old place, but many a toff has found himself there by accident. If a cab driver asks you where you want to go and you say 'Kennington' in the right sort of clipped accent, he's likely to mishear your posh destination as the very un-posh 'Kanning Tunn' and transport you down the East India Dock Road and over the Canning Town fly-over while you try to work out how this is going to get you to Kennington!

A few days after the interview I received a letter from Edward Furness. He wrote: 'Thank you for all you shared in the interview on Wednesday. This letter is to make you the formal offer of the post of Community Worker here at Mayflower, starting work on 31st July, at 9.00am.' The salary was modest, and I would have to pay rent for the one-bedroom flat a few doors down from the Centre.

I was over the moon!

10

Living for the City

The Mayflower Family Centre, in Canning Town, East London, was once described by its most famous Warden—David Sheppard, now Bishop of Liverpool—as 'a situation where we can really meet the sort of person that the church so often doesn't meet at all'.

After his own formative years in an urban area of Merseyside, Roger Sainsbury took over as Warden in 1974. Roger found new ways of taking the church out onto the street, with job creation schemes, a youth and community workers' project, a city farm, and some pioneering outreach work. 'On each Good Friday, we used to re-enact the trial of Jesus in the local market,' says Roger, who for nearly three years was also an alderman on the borough council. 'People who would never normally darken the doors of a church would come along and get very involved with the play. Once, someone telephoned the police to say there was a riot going on.' One year, when the play could not go on, local people jokingly asked why Jesus wasn't coming to Canning Town any more . . .

Roger Sainsbury was succeeded as Warden by Edward Furness—with Peter Watherston arriving as Chaplain at the same time. Roger returned to the East End a few years later as Bishop of Barking. Youth work was in full swing by that point, under Pip Wilson—though the drinking, drug-taking and violence which began to run rife in the club soon resulted in a diminution of the youth work.

'It must have appeared to outsiders that we had closed down many of the areas for which the Mayflower had become known,' says Peter, 'partly because open youth work became impossible—though that isn't a permanent state of affairs. In the long term, all the buildings will be fully used again, though often in a different way to that intended.'

An advice desk, nursery school, sports facilities and a lunch club for the elderly (attracting about forty pensioners per day) have continued to run for many years, and when I joined the staff, these had recently been joined by the innovative New Hunt launderette.

In 1985 the Bass Charrington brewery sold the Mayflower a local pub—now renamed The New Hunt and converted into a coffee bar cum launderette—which has proved extremely popular with the local population. The New Hunt has become a vital focal point of communal life in the area. It was opened without an outside appointment of professional staff, and has always been operated by dedicated people from the Mayflower working voluntarily, in spite of the massive people-power commitment.

The residential accommodation above The New Hunt has been converted into a much-needed hostel for ex-prisoners who have made a Christian commitment. Doreen Turner, a member of the Mayflower leadership team, ran a pilot project there in preparation for the opening of the Mayflower's second major project—the conversion of a disused part of the Mayflower complex into a residential place of healing and sanctuary which, in conjunction with some former staff accommodation, was intended to offer fourteen bedrooms. It opened a few years after I arrived.

I vividly remember my first day at the Mayflower, set in the petrol-scented air and noise-polluted environment of south-west Newham. I walked around the corner on the modern estate that has sprung up around the Centre—replacing the bomb sites that had scarred the landscape till well into the 1960s—and there was the red brick building, with its mock Tudor bits, and its anonymous youth club building tacked on the side. About the first thing I saw was a large rat coming out of some rubbish on the steps by the back entrance! (I'm glad I've seen no more since!)

The morning began with a vigorous prayer session—then I was thrown in the deep end. Edward Furness asked me to go onto the advice desk, and I protested that I didn't know how to give advice! I had thought that I was going to be trained first, but Edward smiled his warm, reassuring smile and said, 'You'll be all right.'

My first client was an Irish woman, and everything *wasn't* all right! She needed specific advice on a particular problem, and to my acute embarrassment, I couldn't provide it. I hadn't a clue what she should do. She burst out crying, while I sat there with a profound feeling of helplessness.

I helped out with the lunch club that day, and got on a lot better. A smile for the old ladies, and a good dollop of creamy custard and they were well pleased. Since then, I've never looked back!

I had arrived in the middle of a big dispute with the local council. For many years, the Mayflower had received substantial council grants to pay for many of its workers, but now the London Borough of Newham was holding a 'witch hunt' to make sure that all organisations which benefited from its generous funding were 'politically correct'. I spent some time 'putting my face around' and getting known by the other voluntary and statutory bodies in the borough, and quickly noticed a strong emphasis on the promotion of homosexuality, lesbianism, equal opportunities, minority faiths, sexual equality, and the rest of the 'right-on' left-wing agenda.

I was asked by a Newham employee how the Mayflower would respond to a request for an Islamic group to study the Qu'ran on its premises, or to allow lesbian groups to have assertiveness classes there. I pointed out that the Mayflower was a Christian Centre and that some activities might therefore be deemed inappropriate. It was a purely hypothetical situation designed to 'set me up', and the official looked suitably indignant about my cautious answer. Next I knew, the word was going round that the Mayflower was sexist and racist, and we were going to have all our grants cut. Specifically, the grant which was intended to pay my wages was going to be stopped.

Canning Town was starting to look more inhospitable than many of the torrid countries rampant with dangerous wildlife that I had visited during my travelling days!

Some lobbying was carried out at Newham Town Hall, several councillors looked very sheepish, and the grant was allowed—but only for one further year. It was a relief that the Mayflower was no longer answerable to Newham Council, and from then onwards my salary was raised from outside trusts.

My predecessor had been very involved with local politics, but the Mayflower and I saw my role as more ground level work, visiting the sick and elderly and integrating my way into the deprived and vulnerable sections of Canning Town's multi-racial community. The advice desk is open on three days a week, offering basic benefit advice. I also counsel people, praying with those who want spiritual help. I'm involved with Age Concern, befriending elderly people who have just come out of hospital.

One old man had an outside toilet, no hot or cold water, and a damp bedroom. He wouldn't have survived another winter there, so I helped to get the council to remedy the situation. They put him into a luxuriously refurbished sheltered home, Terry Waite House, with regular care and entertainment. He attended our church services for a while.

Another old lady whom I used to visit regularly, fell over while trying to use her commode and soiled herself. I had to climb in through a window and help her to clean herself up.

My job entails bringing the love of Jesus Christ into the local community in a sensitive and practical way. One chap came in to the advice desk, sat down and said, 'I'm an alcoholic. Will you help me?' He wanted to get away from his family to rehabilitate; we were able to find him a place where he could go and dry out. Another client broke down in tears of joy, because she was so relieved to find someone who was prepared to give her help. Above all, my job involves being a *practical* witness to the Christian faith, now that I have come fully to grips with my task.

The elders of Romford Community Church gave me money from church funds to help me with my removal expenses, to become a 'missionary' in deep, dark Canning Town! They expressed concern upon hearing that I would be moving church as well as home, but it was essential that I worship at the Mayflower if I was to become fully a part of the local community.

For several years now the Mayflower's worshipping community has comprised largely single people and divorcees, with few nuclear families with children. We have sought to be an extended family, helping one another in our individual shortcomings and deficiencies. An almost complete breakdown in family life has occurred in Canning Town; and some people have been through break ups more than once.

One local family, in a debt crisis and likely to be evicted at any moment, began attending our services. They were very welcome since, though their marriage was rocky, they were one of the few married couples in the congregation. Unfortunately, the wife then ran off, leaving behind eight children. It was a painful time, but as a church, we pulled together to help.

On another occasion, the church was able to help a woman with debt problems, by letting her live in a local house owned by Edward Furness. Unfortunately, she formed a relationship with a local married man, and the Mayflower needed to exercise church discipline. In the end, the man became violent with her, and the police were called. The woman and her children had to be found a 'safe house' by the Mayflower, before the council resettled her in another borough.

These stories typify the hopelessness with which some local people move from one relationship to another, desperately seeking one which will work for them, and declining advice from those who can plainly see the sorrow that lies ahead. Clearly my own background—and growing counselling skills—well equipped me to try to help those trapped in vicious cycles of behaviour so close to those I had previously known. I have struggled to make people understand the consequences of their own actions, and to realise that Christ is the only stable foundation for human relations.

I completed a basic ten-week counselling course, and learnt how to get people to talk about their problems and to answer their own questions. Later, I completed courses for those who have suffered loss, and one on how to counsel relatives of murder victims. Coming to terms with one's own experiences is a vital part of the process of becoming a good counsellor, so the training has paid dividends in my own life.

Sadly, I am often called upon (as a volunteer with Victim Support) to counsel traumatised victims of crime, of which there are very many in a gritty urban borough like Newham. Transport is another of my areas, and I co-ordinate the drivers and transport which bring people into our lunch club. When the youth work started up again in 1992, I went along on a voluntary basis to lend a hand.

Workers have to be very careful when counselling female clients. I might conduct a first interview with a woman who came in, but I would very quickly refer her to a woman staff member if she appeared to be suffering from an emotional problem, or needed prolonged counselling.

It was at the Mayflower that I finally conquered my own lust problem. Peter and Hannah Watherston prayed with me that I would be delivered from my 'roving eye'. I came to realise, through counselling and prayer with Peter, that lust for women was an idol to which I was still bowing down. I smashed the idol for good, and broke its influence over me.

The first year at Canning Town was tough, and I often felt out on a limb. There were no other men of my age or background to befriend, or with whom to socialise. Moving from a house which had been a family home to an empty one-bedroom flat, situated next-door to the Centre, also took some acclimatisation. I remember receiving a phone call from an old friend, who refused to drive into Canning Town, for fear that his car would be stolen!

Quite often when I tell people that I live in Canning Town, they respond with a look that is midway between sympathy and amazement. I often feel tempted to add mockingly, 'I was mugged five times last week, and that was by church members!' There is, of course, a criminal fraternity in Canning Town, ranging from organised 'firms' (gangs) to petty thieving, dealing with 'off the back of a lorry' items. It's common for people not only to work and 'sign on' for income support at the same time, but to regard this as morally justified!

But not all of Canning Town's colourful population indulge in violence, crime and degradation. Not all Canning Town teenagers are rough, cheeky and violent. They are ordinary kids who can be offensive at times, but no more so than kids everywhere, regardless of background or class. Sadly, Canning Town residents have a reputation that counts against them when applying for jobs or bank loans.

For about a year, I helped to run the youth club, catering for around sixty 11–14-year-olds, of whom only half a dozen qualified as foul-mouthed bullies, ready to form their own gangs. This handful caused so much disruption that a visit to their parents was necessary. But the proud parents could not accept that their 'little angels' had done wrong. I wished that I could play them a videotape of their offspring at the youth club!

Living at the Mayflower has been like living on the frontline of a spiritual and moral battlefield; it's challenging and character-building work, a make-or-break situation. Living in the inner city has been the toughest journey of them all. Canning Town is a depressing and neglected urban priority area, though working here has its satisfactions. One has to get to grips with issues more quickly than in suburban areas. (Which is not to say that suburban areas don't have problems of their own.) I'm grateful for the lessons I've learned here, and for the powerful opportunities I've had to minister to desperate people. Often there have been too few workers and too much work. But there have been many joys, too; and the view from the top deck of my 'heaven-bound bus' has not always been bleak.

The local church has become the heart and hub of the activities which have developed in the Mayflower facilities. A morning congregation averaging 25–30 and an evening congregation of 40–50 reflects a slight growth in recent years. Instead of being passively on the receiving end of outside help, East End Christians are now able to help people from both inside and outside the tightly-knit local community who are facing serious problems. Local Christians have become a valuable spiritual resource to be used on a wider basis.

The Mayflower's innovative Sanctuary project began with a passionate desire to help needy people, prior to any thought of opening a hostel. We were unsure who would actually come, but some of our buildings naturally lend themselves to being a residential Sanctuary, because of the garden at the centre, the character of the Mayflower buildings themselves, the leisure facilities we can provide, and the community that is developing here. We opened in late 1992, and have had many desperate and needy people to stay, sometimes just for a few nights and sometimes for several months, depending upon the specific need.

I first heard about the Reachout Trust through meeting Doug Harris at the Spring Harvest Christian teaching holiday, in 1990. The organisation exists to reach out to people who have been ensnared by pseudo-Christian cults and sects. My memories of being a member of the Unification Church came flooding back. Was there some way in which I could help others who had been similarly misled by the 'Moonies' and who had yet to find their way out of the darkness?

I asked for more information, and was given some literature by Doug. Later, I attended a weekend of informative and instructive seminars, mainly given by people who had themselves been entangled in a cult. Doug originally set up Reachout to evangelise Jehovah's Witnesses and Mormons. His brief was now much wider, and many experiences I have had with Buddhism, feminist theology and the New Age were relevant to the work of Reachout Trust. After a few months of praying and seeking God's confirmation, I became the Reachout Area Director for East London. I was to receive referrals to counsel and befriend cult victims who had come out or who had begun to question their leaders but were afraid to come out because of the family pressures and the fear of judgement.

I could relate, in a small way, to the pressures they are under from my time as a 'Moonie'. If your whole family and social network is wrapped up in a cult, to come out of it forces you to change your entire existence and to find your own way in life, without a friend in the world.

Perhaps the biggest problem for many spiritually-parched people living in the spiritual barrenness of the inner city is the *powerlessness* that vulnerable people feel, in having no control over their own lives. It is that lack of power which often makes them easy targets for cults and sects which promise—but don't deliver—dignity to the downtrodden, and hope to the helpless.

Damp and overcrowded, but spiritually empty and dry, Cranbrook Point was home for one impoverished family for whom I arranged an appeal. Within a week they were rehoused in the area where they most wanted to live. The female partner jubilantly came round to my tiny office straight away, waving the keys, in a deliriously happy daze.

People often feel that they have to buy their way to God. I was introduced to a young man called Norris, who was a member of the Central London Church of Christ (they have now shortened their name). Norris was becoming increasingly disillusioned, from the pressure he was under by the leadership, to commit all his spare time to persuading people to attend Church of Christ meetings. Members were also expected to give all their spare cash, and savings, to the COC, though Norris feared that much of the money was going directly into the leaders' pockets.

It became clear as we talked that Norris was being crippled emotionally by a deep sense of guilt, because he was simply too exhausted—trying to be an evangelist on top of a full-time job—to 'deliver the goods' adequately. His words brought back memories of my experiences of the Unification Church, particularly the fear of 'committing spiritual suicide' by leaving an institution that claims to be God's only true church. It seemed as though the Church of Christ was competing with the Jehovah's Witnesses, the Mormons and the 'Moonies' to be the only path to eternal life with God!

I prayed with Norris that he would break free from the emotional blackmail, and no longer feel condemned by a 'God' who seemed more like a cosmic bogie man than the gentle carpenter of Galilee. I asked God to bless him with the reassurance that he was loved, valued and accepted for *who he was*, and not for *what he could do*. He told me that no one had ever before prayed like that for him. The prayers he had known in the Church of Christ were always the harsh self-condemnations of those striving to do better.

Norris struggled with feelings of guilt and condemnation for several weeks before finally accepting that he had been set free by Christ's death on the cross. Norris' debt to God had been paid on the nail, and the Holy Spirit was waiting to lead him straight into the forgiving arms of his loving heavenly Father. Norris is now an active member of St John's, Stratford—an evangelical Church of England congregation.

Religion and people get mixed up. When we think of religions, we don't think of theology and doctrine so much as the people of those faiths whom we meet. I've met Muslims, Hindus and Buddhists—and 'Moonies' and JWs for that matter—who are deeply spiritual people, but though there are elements of truth in all established world religions, I believe that *the fullness and culmination of them lies in Jesus Christ.*

Seeing people realise that, and enter into the kingdom of light, makes everything worthwhile.

East London is rife with interest in the occult. There are spiritualist churches and exotic New Age bookshops all over the place. In Newham, there are frequent occult fairs, where astrologers and tarot readers ply their trade. The weird end of alternative medicine is also heavily represented in the East End. One local Hindu-styled group is led by a woman who claims to be the incarnation of Christ. My first-hand experiences of Hinduism and Buddhism in India and Thailand come in useful occasionally, particularly on the Mayflower advice desk, and in my hospital visits.

After I'd been at the Mayflower for a couple of years, I came across an intriguing circular asking for Christian volunteers to join the chaplaincy team at Newham General Hospital. I was the first person to be interviewed, and the first person to join the team, whose role is to provide spiritual and emotional support to both staff and patients. The Revd Linda Steward, the full-time chaplain, took me on reluctantly at first—she was afraid that my fundamentalist evangelical stance would make me insensitive towards patients' needs, particularly those of other faiths. No worries! I'd seen enough 'hard sell' evangelistic tactics to appreciate her concern, but fundamentalism does not always have to be equated with fanaticism.

Since I'd become a Christian, I was gradually learning to be sensitive to people, particularly those of other faiths and orientations. I worship a God of grace and, though I believe that he is found most fully in Christianity, I recognise that other faiths also give glimpses of him. I have come to learn to have gentle dialogue with those outside the Christian tradition about their own faith. This has proved particularly the case with many of the patients I have met on my hospital rounds. Starting late in 1990, I began going into the hospital for one morning a week, gradually learning my way around this strange world of syringes and stethoscopes, bottles and bedpans. It was my privilege to befriend and comfort both the patients who made speedy recoveries, and the terminally ill.

For six months, I spent an hour or so each week with a lady named Margaret, in her early sixties and dying of leukaemia. She initially decided to refuse any therapy—reluctant to put herself through unnecessary pain and suffering when her survival prospects were so slim and she had outlived her sell-by date, as she quipped. But later she changed her mind, and fought for her life. We spoke often of spiritual matters, and she gave me 'unspoken' permission to talk with her about Jesus. She was quite a lady. An overzealous former member of the chaplaincy team gave her a hellfire and brimstone sermon, but, in spite of her obvious disgust, Margaret kept her dignity and responded politely to the onslaught. No doubt he had her salvation at heart, but he was unable to share his faith with tact and gentleness. It was my privilege to give the valedictory address at her funeral—and, at the crematorium, to press the button to send her casket into the furnace.

It has been challenging to me to work through doubts and the sense of loss felt by many of the people with whom I have briefly conversed. I remember meeting a young mother who had just given birth. There were many complications, and she died a couple of days later; but in that short time, I tried to share with her as best I could, and to try to catch an insight into her own perspective.

It was through experiences like these that I came to know God's healing in my own life. He has healed me of past wounds, such as seeing my mother die of cancer. He has set me free to do his will, and shown me the reality of his love at a very deep level—though I have still had to work through times of doubt, particularly about divine physical healing of the terminally ill.

I've sometimes thought: If I had faith even the size of a mustard seed, I should be able to lay hands on people and see them walk away from their death bed. Was I being faithless in not allowing God to use me in this way? There have been frustrating moments when I have doubted both God's omnipotent power and his lack of benevolence. But even though I have walked along the knife-edge of doubt, I have never fallen. I don't consider it unhealthy to have doubts, so long as they are shared and prayed through with a mature Christian friend.

Sometimes patients have helped me more than I have been able to help them. The work has helped to ground me in my own faith and to work through my own loss. It has been tough at times, and if I wasn't constantly upheld by God's strength and peace, there is no way that I could do the job. *I enjoy the work.*

Often people are dying and turn to me for answers to the unanswerable questions of life and death. Why do some people have to suffer when they seem never to have done anything to deserve such pain? I often find myself asking that. But whether we live to be nine or ninety, it is still a mere blink by comparison with living for ever—as Christ promises to those who accept him as their Lord. I'm seen by many to be 'God's representative', and that's an awesome responsibility. Many times I've been called vicar, reverend, father or padre, and been expected to have all the solutions to every spiritual problem. *I don't!* In fact I've always been cautious about presenting a pat answer to the dying.

It would be a cheap move to exploit their uncertainty in order to gain thrilling death-bed conversions. This is particularly true of the gay men whom I've talked with, counselled, and prayed for as they lay dying from AIDS-related illnesses. I will tell them about God, and pray with them, but I would never exploit their weakness—and the lack of choices that comes on the verge of death—by pressing the gospel message upon them if they really didn't want to hear it. Often I come away wondering if I've done the right thing.

Newham is a richly cosmopolitan community, and being a world traveller helps at times. 'Oh, you come from Rajastan?' I say. 'I've been there! Whereabouts? Oh, is that little grocery shop still there by the railway station?' It certainly breaks down a lot of barriers!

I find I can often vividly relate to their diverse experiences because they find echoes in my own life. But I would never say 'I know what you're going through,' because these things are different for each person. I empathise, never sympathise.

One middle-aged family man I remember, was originally from the Gujarat. He went to Kenya on business, was vaccinated against malaria out there, and contracted AIDS from the unsterilised needle. I saw him shortly after the diagnosis, when his Hindu faith was proving inadequate to help him to cope with the shock. He had his *Bhagavad Gita* with him. I knew enough about its contents to swing the conversation firmly around to religion, and to share my own faith with him. He was deeply moved when I began to pray with him; he put his hand on my shoulder and began to cry softly. As I stood up, he took my breath away by trying to touch my feet—a sign of deep respect usually given to a family elder or a 'holy man'.

A year later, I saw him in hospital. His skin pigmentation was changing and he was covered in blotches. His eyesight was failing, but he recognised me and we shook hands. He mentioned how much my prayers had meant to him, and I again gently shared with him my own conviction that Jesus Christ is the only way to God. We spoke of Krishna and the *Bhagavad Gita* and entered into meaningful dialogue, respecting each other's views.

I've come across many tragic people who have tried to take their own life. One was a guy called James. I was asked to speak to this cynical and exuberant Scotsman by the hospital staff, as he lay in his hospital bed with drips in his arm, surrounded by clipboards, monitors and other medical paraphernalia; and we got on like long-lost brothers straight away.

'There was one part of me wanting to be there to get rid of the pain, the other wanting to get out so that I could try again thinking of other ways of killing myself,' James remembers. When I sat down with him, James' first impression of me was, 'Oh no, not another stupid trainee nurse or student doctor come to ask me silly questions. This is all I need. Well, I might as well answer his questions—it passes the time.'

He had taken an almighty dose of paracetamol that could have killed a whale, but he had lived through the experience. I think he'd mixed the tablets with other drugs which had caused him to be sick. Together with the high tolerance his body had built up, this saved him from the chronic liver failure that would otherwise have killed him.

James explained that he was depressed and homeless, sleeping on the floor with friends and relatives, but basically eking out a very lonely existence. His wasn't a cry for help, he'd been quite serious about wanting to die. I shared Jesus with him, hoping to show him something worth living for. He showed little enthusiasm, but he wasn't disinterested.

Later I suggested that James could perhaps move into the Sanctuary. The staff prayed about it and decided unanimously that they would be prepared to accept him. I explained to James that here was somewhere he could be cared for and looked after, and he jumped at the opportunity. Without this offer, he would have been on the streets.

A few months later, he committed his life to Jesus. It has not been an easy transition for him into the Christian life, but like all of us at the Mayflower, he is learning how to trust God and to live with him. He has since served on the *Anastasis* mercy ship, helping on the engineering side, as a means of turning his faith into practical action.

11

'I Married a Monster from Outer Space!'

In 1990, I attended a ten-week course at the Newham Parents' Centre, one evening per week, learning to be a better counsellor. It was a course run by the London Borough of Newham, and I was the only Christian present at each of the two-hour sessions. I was one of the few men present, too, among the ten or so participants.

My attitude towards women had changed drastically since I had become a follower of Christ. I treated my fellow counselling students as sisters now, and not as potential conquests. By this time, my waistline had begun to expand a bit and I was starting to develop a double chin. At least my dark brown hair had not shown signs of falling out or going grey! I made a point of keeping fit, and always 'worked out' regularly, three times per week. Nevertheless, I looked far from the young stud that I had been a decade earlier.

I didn't mind. I felt comfortable with myself as I slouched almost horizontal in my chair, casually dressed and trying not to yawn too much at the duller parts of the teaching. I was very laid back about the course, often making people laugh through my clowning around. My sense of humour often came to the fore in small group situations like this.

Among the many practical exercises we had to split into twos and discuss various topics. One of those topics was 'sex before marriage', and I made it clear to the confident fair-haired woman sitting opposite me that this was something in which I no longer believed. I also managed to tell her about Jesus and give her my testimony—all within the space of the two minutes (it was timed) that we each had to communicate our views to the other.

This sassy woman knew just where she stood on most topics, but she warmed when I mentioned the name of Jesus. It transpired that she was a fairly radical feminist, who had become keenly interested in religion.

'I've been looking into different religions for quite some time,' she explained. 'I'm particularly interested in feminist theology.' She had learned a bit about Catholicism, and was curious to know something about the views of the evangelical church. Very inquisitive, she had a battery of penetrating questions. I quite enjoyed chatting with her.

A week or two later *she* asked *me* out for a drink. Actually, she claimed to have invited the whole counselling group down to the pub, but that I was the only one who could make it!

Anyway, we found ourselves sitting in The Boleyn pub, a typical East End pub, perhaps less noisy than some, with most of its fine original Edwardian interior intact. We were both drinking pints of beer, and I noticed that she was more than keeping up with me. Yet there was nothing forced, embittered or aggressive about her extrovert character; she behaved warmly, like 'a good mate' with a bubbly personality, rather than a stereotypical man-eating feminist; though she did wear shabby denim dungarees.

Warning bells began to ring for me when she described some of the feminist theology meetings which she had attended. They sounded very occult! There was no 'drawing down the moon' or any of the other explicit forms of witchcraft but the heavy emphasis on the Earth Goddess gave strong hints about the pagan origins of this movement.

She shared with me the great fears she felt about the established church with its patriarchal system, but responded positively when I warned her that she was perhaps dabbling on the fringes of witchcraft.

'I wasn't aware of that,' she said. I shared the gospel with her very positively, and she didn't seem too put off.

'I've long been politically a feminist,' she explained, 'and when I became interested in spirituality in the mid-eighties, I tried to marry the two by delving into feminist theology.' She confirmed that there was a pre-Christian faction within feminist theology, who were very goddess orientated; though there are Christian feminists, too, who seek to 'feminise the church'. These people tend to veer towards creation-centred spirituality, which is a long way from the Bible-based evangelical tradition.

She was excellent company, lively and alert. It transpired that her father had been a major in the army, and as a child she had travelled abroad with his different postings.

'We've got a lot in common,' she said as I told her about my travelling days. She too had spent time in Cairo, not bumming around as I had done, but teaching English. Unlike me, she had been to university—studying English and American Literature at the University of Kent at Canterbury, and she had trained as a teacher before going abroad to teach in Finland, Egypt and Italy.

Sue, her name was: Sue Boyes. She was slim, and she had one of those faces that can make its owner look a naive teenager one minute and a worldly-wise, mature intellectual the next. Her character was forceful without being domineering, and she was as bright and sharp as a razor blade.

She lived in the heart of an Asian community up Green

Street, a mile or two from the Mayflower, so I invited her around for a meal the next Friday—intent on taking her to church on the Sunday afterwards. I didn't feel threatened by her, but I knew I could be in for a challenging time. I certainly wasn't going to be bored with *this* young lady.

I cooked my 'special' rice, with fresh prawns thrown in, opened a bottle of wine and settled down. I played her a tape of a song I had written and recorded with Bob Cranham—'Travelling Man'—but she was unimpressed! We soon got around to talk of spiritual matters, and began to feel comfortable together.

Sue had been asking questions about Christianity for several years, and like me she had often burned the midnight oil in long talks about religious faith. She had explored the New Age movement, meditation, mysticism, Buddhism and a heap of other doctrines, and was friendly with an older Catholic gentleman.

We saw each other regularly, and although the relationship didn't become overtly sexual, we were soon more than platonic friends. After only five days, I felt positive that we had clicked. What did she have that my dozens of other girlfriends didn't have? I haven't a clue! Perhaps I felt that she understood me more, or maybe it was just my nesting instincts coming to the fore. But I know that God brought us together.

I wrote to another girl I had been seeing occasionally, to say that I wouldn't be seeing her again because I had met Sue. A second girl I'd recently asked out was also left on the sidelines. It wasn't as though I was desperate, or that I had no other options, but something felt right between Sue and me.

'I hope that one day you might become my wife,' I said, realising that there was no way that I would ever marry a girl who wasn't a Christian. I hoped that God was going to get his skates on here! Sue was a little shocked, because the idea of marriage wasn't something to which she was accustomed. She was more used to people simply living together.

Sue was still very anxious about the patriarchal nature of the institutionalised church, and it was only with great reluctance that she first came along to the Mayflower. I was grateful for the support we both received from Peter Watherston and his wife, Hannah. Between us, we were able to answer lots of the questions Sue had had for many years. Before we met, she had considered joining a feminist community, because she was in love with the whole idea of a living community of people with a shared purpose. The Mayflower's community-orientated ideals appealed to her in many ways.

There were a fair number of problems to sort out for both of us. Sue had been in several long-term relationships before, so we were both carrying a lot of emotional baggage from our respective pasts. The months that followed were not easy.

We were having a meal once, and her Catholic gentleman friend phoned up for a chat. For about forty-five minutes she talked animatedly to him on the telephone. Afterwards, I protested that it was bad manners to do this when she had invited me around, and we were in the middle of eating. She accused me of being jealous, but I protested my innocence. The atmosphere was tense for a few minutes, but the matter soon blew over.

In our different ways, we both lacked certain social graces. I was more an 'egg'n'chips' sort of bloke than a 'scampi'n'quiche' fellow, her friends pointed out. Some of Sue's acquaintances also commented negatively about my lack of feminist awareness and my poor education, making out that my IQ was just about on a par with that of a potted plant!

'People are amazed that I am going out with someone like you, Gordon,' she told me. 'It's certainly challenging many of my friends, because you're not a "new man".' I didn't even know what a 'new man' was!

Sue took several months to come to terms with the emotional consequences of having been across the world and missing out on a settled way of life. And could I share the full details of my own earlier lifestyle—the way I'd emotionally abused women through so many relationships? Might that make it difficult for this new partnership to work? How would Sue react? But gradually we sorted things out, and neither of us held anything back.

Sue had not long been back in Britain and she confessed to having felt a little lonely before meeting up with me. There were certain family tensions disturbing her, too, but she was beginning to get her act together after being out of the country for six years. She had missed out on most of the Thatcherite years and had returned to find Britain very cold and soulless. She was spiritually parched and responded warmly to my talk about Jesus. But she fought shy of making any firm commitment.

She went off to Pilgrim's Hall one weekend, and while she was there she fell into several long conversations with my old friends Peter and Pat Garrett, and was seriously challenged by the claims of Christ. Peter brought her to the very edge of commitment.

'I'm not quite ready yet,' she said, to which Peter Garrett responded, 'Well when *are* you going to be ready?' That simple question was the breakthrough, and Sue resolved to become a follower of Christ, there and then. I was over the moon when she told me!

'There was a very long period when I struggled to sort out my relationship with God,' Sue remembers. 'I was very wary of men, too, so Gordon had a hard job courting me. Perhaps I would have become a Christian without meeting Gordon; I had been to various churches, and even a Quaker Meeting House during my search. I had lived with a born-again Christian woman in Cairo for nearly three years, but her faith had never seemed right for me. If I'd come to Christ without meeting Gordon, though, I think I would have been a much more liberal Christian.'

Sue moved into a house with three other Christians who helped to support her in her new faith. These three flat mates came out with Sue and me to celebrate her birthday, shortly before Christmas 1990, and watched as I gave Sue a diamond engagement ring as her birthday present. She hadn't expected any formal engagement, and was very surprised that I had bothered to do something quite so 'establishment' as to buy a ring.

Sue and I are very different in many ways, but compatible. Sue is very discerning, able to pinpoint specific issues. She thinks things through better than I do. It wasn't easy, given our respective backgrounds, to refrain from full sexual intercourse before marriage—but we did refrain. Common strengths lay in our shared counselling abilities, but Christ was the firm anchor of our relationship.

We were in love, but there were many fraught moments on the way to the aisle. Sue felt reluctant to move into my pokey one-bedroom flat once we were married, perceiving that this was my space that she was invading. She felt she might feel suffocated by being so close to the Mayflower. Sue also required much counselling from Hannah Watherston, to overcome the accumulated hurts of thirty years of living.

Then, three months before our wedding was due to take place, Sue called it all off. I'll let her explain in her own words: 'It was so incongruous us being together in the first place. I don't agree with all of Gordon's thinking. My emotional needs hadn't been met by the Catholic guy I had been seeing, but Gordon was able to address those deeply felt needs. He is more stable and solid than I am—and often more emotionally mature.

'I had often tried to get out of the relationship. I think I was testing him, to find out how serious he was, and to see whether he could really handle all the emotional garbage I was throwing at him. I would have been happier if we could have run away and had a quiet wedding, but there was pressure from the Mayflower—because my fiancé was the community worker there—to have a big do for the whole Mayflower community.

'I was a bit "culture shocked" through being a new Christian, and I was worried that being married to Gordon would make me a square peg in a round hole. That's why I called it all off.'

But a few weeks later the wedding was back on, and we married one bright August day in 1991, with the Mayflower chapel packed with guests. I really warmed to Sue's father, who gave a lively speech at the reception. 'My daughter's gone and married a southerner!' he exclaimed in mock disgust.

Now I was no longer alone; there were two of us travelling together, towards the same heavenly destination.

As it turned out, the issues we thought might be problematic were not difficulties at all. Sue has pursued her own career, teaching language skills to immigrant and refugee children and adults, and has remained her own person. We can both get irritable, because we stretch ourselves quite a lot; but it's the same for any couple.

We are both very independent people, so we have to be careful not to be too possessive towards one another. We accept that each can go out with his or her own circle of friends occasionally, but we are each secure with the other in our relationship, and we don't feel threatened by anyone else. We know that no one else is going to come between us, and we feel safe and comfortable with each other. We have been able to sort out the compromises needed to respect each other's interests and attitudes.

How is sex different within the context of marriage, compared with sex during my wild and promiscuous youth? Many young people find sex attractive because it runs counter to values that are now often seen as old fashioned. It can often seem very exciting for young lovers to perform the sex act in the back of a car or at a parental home where there is some risk of being caught. For a married couple in their own home, it's respectable and there is no chance of interruption—at least until children come along. But by emphasising the sex act itself and not the relationship within which it takes place, the permissive society encourages single people to miss out on the important aspects of making love which are only found within a stable and permanent union: having someone to wake up with in the morning; having someone who is 'always there for you'; knowing that there is one person who always puts *you* first (after God); and sharing each other's lives—not just each other's bodies. Marriage is first and foremost about commitment.

Christ's followers often seem to be so concerned that sex shouldn't happen before marriage that they often fail to explain how rewarding physical intercourse can be within the sanctity of marriage. It's something that doesn't usually get talked about too much from the pulpit, and there is too little guidance for Christians with sexual problems. The church is perhaps in danger of stressing only the negative aspects of sex, rather than emphasising the joy of creative passion, the thrill of a man and wife exploring each other's bodies and discovering the secrets of what 'turns each other on'.

I think most Christians would condemn anything which leads to permissiveness, but too often we forget that sex is one of God's greatest gifts. It is not intended simply for procreation, but also for enjoyment and for the bonding of a relationship. Sex is a good thing which only turns bad when it is misused.

Perhaps the risk of marital breakdown would be lessened if pastors were encouraged, in the right circumstances, to talk to church members about sex. When a couple have problems, and keep them bottled up, that can gnaw like a cancer at a marriage. Talk is the best sex therapy, and Christians need to be stressing the need to be more experimental and to truly get to know one another. We might be seen then as more than just interfering old fuddy-duddies.

Sex is a very important part of marriage, but it's not the most important. Love, warmth, communication and cuddles are more important. Sex is portrayed in the media as the be-all and end-all, which it isn't—at its best it is a bonus. Understanding, patience, compromise and humour are the ingredients that make a good marriage.

My attitude to women has certainly altered significantly since coming to know the Lord Jesus. God opened up areas of my personality and character that I had kept hidden since my mother's death. I was never violent towards the opposite sex, but my motivation was usually less than desirable. My attitude changed dramatically as my relationship with God evolved.

I have repented of my old nature, and I struggle to become a true 'new man' of God, putting the world's ways behind me. I used to be a right so-and-so, but I've been forgiven by God's grace, and he has made me able to relate properly to women; able to give and to receive real love. And for that I am eternally grateful.

12

A Sort of Homecoming

As the years have gone by, thoughts about my natural mother and father have seldom entered my head. It was my adoptive parents whom I regarded as my real mum and dad, and they were both dead. No one could ever replace them, so what good would it have done me to trace my natural parents?

But late in 1990, I went along to Catherine House, Kingsway, to try to collect a copy of my original birth certificate. The Adoption Act 1976 had been introduced to allow adopted adults to have access to details about their natural family, and I was curious to discover my original name. I was interviewed by a civil servant, who gave me a form to complete, explaining that it would cost me £5, and that I would soon be on my way to knowing who I really was.

By this stage in my life, I already knew the real me. I'd been going out with Sue for a couple of months, I was settled in at the Mayflower, I knew and was known by the eternal God. What else did I need to know about myself? I was comfortable with being Gordon Barley, and I couldn't see how having a copy of my original birth certificate would change anything. It would be just an academic exercise to collect this bit of paper which would reveal something of my life before adoption. I've never been fond of academic exercises, though. The form sat on a shelf for a couple of months till I could be bothered to deal with it.

Then, one Saturday, as I came back to the flat after a busy day, I picked up a long brown envelope laying in the hallway. It was addressed to my adoptive parents at the old house, and had been forwarded on to me. It looked like one of those social services circulars, so I didn't really pay it too much attention. I put the kettle on for a cup of tea, slit open the envelope and began to read the letter inside.

'Dear Mr and Mrs Barley,' it began. 'This is about your adopted son, Gordon. His natural sister, Jenny, wishes to make contact with him . . . '

I think my jaw must have hit the floor at that point. This was the first I knew that I even *had* a sister called Jenny.

I phoned up the Tower Hamlets social worker who had written the letter, to be told 'She's not in.' I tried again later. 'She's still not in.' Later . . . still no luck. Eventually I managed to speak to this person who had written saying 'Please contact me urgently.' And she hadn't a clue who I was!

'You've sent a letter stressing how urgent this is,' I said firmly, 'and yet you can't remember my name.' I was appalled, but eventually she made an appointment for me to go and see her.

I turned up punctually and then had to twiddle my thumbs for an hour or more. In the end, a secretary came along with a folder and said, 'I'm sorry the social worker has been delayed. She has asked me to give you the file relating to your adoption.' Just as the folder was being thrust into my hands, another social worker swept in and asked me who I was waiting to see. The secretary briefly explained the situation.

'Don't give him that file!' said the second social worker, snatching it away. She couldn't believe that a colleague could have been so unprofessional and incompetent as to instruct a secretary simply to hand me the file and leave me to it.

'There are matters on this file that could be devastating to you,' said the second social worker. 'People can walk under buses because of things they discover about their natural parents. I need to take you through it gently.'

We went into an office and she worked through the file gradually, patiently explaining its contents. My natural mother had been neglected herself, it seemed. Put into a children's home at five, she went back to her mother at fifteen, but her mother had remarried and she wasn't wanted any more. I shivered at the thought of the trauma which comes from discovering that you're 'not wanted' by someone to whom you have turned for safety and protection, comfort and love. Not long after her rejection my natural mother had found herself in a mental hospital.

A mass of insecurities, she had met my father and had borne two children by him in rapid succession, of whom I was the second. She had since been used and abused by many men, and had given birth to other offspring unloved by their fathers. In the late fifties, when signs outside many boarding houses frequently read, 'No blacks, no Irish, no single mothers,' her outlook was bleak. Deserted by her lover, she had little option but to put me up for adoption. She was still alive and well, it seemed, and now lived in Stepney, a couple of miles down the road from me. My natural father lived in nearby Whitechapel. I could easily have walked past them in the street many times, without knowing them. What should I do now? This was all too much.

The letter which my sister Jenny had written, that had

triggered this meeting, was lying on the file. When I read it, I discovered that Jenny was attempting to trace *all* her siblings—all of my mother and father's many other children, all my half-brothers and sisters, however many there were. Phew!

The social worker immediately phoned my natural mother. For the first time in more than thirty years, I heard the voice of the woman who had carried me in her womb for nine months. Actually she was effing and blinding every other word! She wanted to know what was going on now, and blamed the social workers for taking away her 'poor little babies' all those years ago.

It took me a while to find my feet. I was off balance and out of sorts for the next few weeks, but once it sank in, I had no great difficulties in coming to terms with the situation. I wistfully wondered what it would have been like if we had all been brought up together as one big happy family.

I contacted Jenny first, since it was she who had instigated the search. She had located a half-sister, Shirley, who had been independently conducting her own search.

Jenny lives out towards Colchester with husband John, and son, James. She arranged to meet me at the nearest railway station, and I caught a train across to see her. What was she going to look like? How were we going to get on? It wasn't hard to recognise her. She was the only one there—looking very nervous and puffing away at a cigarette to calm herself.

We went for a quick drink and a chat, then she took me back to her middle-class suburban home. I hadn't been sure what to expect; all my relations could have been raving lunatics for all I knew. It was reassuring to see that Jenny was quite normal and in full control of her life. We found out about each other's personal life stories, and gradually got to know one another. I'm terrible at keeping in touch with people, but we do continue to phone and meet occasionally.

Jenny managed to track down all of my natural mother's seven children, and arranged a reunion. Unfortunately I had previously arranged to go abroad on holiday, so I missed out on the occasion. When I returned to Britain, I was determined to meet up with all of them.

A meeting was arranged next between my mother and myself. With help from a social worker, a time and date were arranged, and I went around to her council maisonette to meet the woman who had given birth to me.

So it was that, on a summer's evening, I came out of the tube station and walked along the busy Whitechapel Road. Past the colourful shop fronts and the faces of every nationality, I eventually came to her front door. Again, I didn't know what to expect.

A short, stout, unkempt lady in her middle fifties opened the door, and stood looking at me. How do you greet, for the first time, the woman who gave you life?

'Hello,' I heard myself say.

She invited me in, and put the kettle on. I called her by her first name, Flo, because it didn't seem right to call her 'Mother'. My natural mother (I won't call her my *biological* mother because it makes her sound like a soap powder) could never replace the mother who brought me up, treated me as her own son, and who died in 1975. Chain smoking and cussing occasionally, Flo told me about her life. Then she filled me in about the circumstances of my birth and the early days of my own life.

She had been institutionalised from an early age, and had known nothing but rejection since the age of five when she had been sent to a children's home, before being callously committed to an institute for the mentally ill from the age of fifteen. Meeting my father, having two children by him, then having him reject her, pushed her over the edge.

Being discarded and disowned once again, now by her lover, was naturally an experience which left her emotionally shattered, and unable to cope with bringing up a young child.

'I was very much in love with your father,' she told me. 'His name was Marco. Around the time you were born, he was doing nine months himself, in Wormwood Scrubs. I took you in to see him as a babe in arms.' She had been nervous about this meeting with me after so many years, but she was very self-controlled.

Marco had been unfaithful to her. Partly as a way of getting back at him, she married another man—with the unlikely surname Squelch—while young Marco was serving time, and while she was pregnant with me. The marriage only lasted for a few months, though this man's name appears—incorrectly—on my original birth certificate as my father. If I had seen that birth certificate when I had first made application for it several months earlier, I would quite naturally—and wrongly—have assumed that Mr Squelch was my physical father. I was glad that my mother was there to clarify the matter.

Of course, after the end of her marriage, the relationship between Marco and Flo was long over, and Flo drifted into other relationships. The fruits of those brief unions are her other children. Tina (my full sister), Sandra, Jenny, Shirley, Dennis and Billy, in that order.

None of us looks like any of the others. Some are tall, some are short, some are fat and some are thin. We come in all shapes and sizes, even those with the same father. Tina, the eldest, has the same father as me, and the two youngest—the only ones brought up by Flo herself—share the same sire. Over the weeks and months that followed, I met and got to know them all. They are all really nice people. Tina and I discovered that we once used to drink in the same pub. Dennis became a volunteer escort on the Mayflower's lunch club service, before replacing the driver as a paid employee, and I am now his boss!

There are a similar number of legitimate siblings, if not more, on my father's side, and probably many more born 'the other side of the blanket', Flo told me. I had a meal with her that first time, and she later came over to my flat to eat with Sue and me. She continues to apologise for having rejected me: 'There was nowhere for me to go, and I wanted the best for you. I wanted to keep in touch with you, but they wouldn't let me.' She retains a hatred for all social workers. 'Were you well looked after?' It must be a terrible guilt to have given a child up for adoption.

Initially, she started calling me 'Marco', and I had to keep correcting her. Apparently, I looked the dead spit of my father when he was my age. Then she started referring to my wife as 'Pat', the name of the woman for whom Marco left Flo, and whom he subsequently married.

I wondered if Flo subconsciously saw Sue as 'the other woman'—a rival for her son's affections. Sue couldn't handle it when she discovered who 'Pat' was; she bolted out the door, and her relationship with Flo was very cool for months afterwards.

Flo has now paired up with another man, a neighbour who is the salt of the earth, and her maisonette is very well kept. She has now been able to pull her life together.

My telephone rang one evening. When I picked up the receiver, a voice with a stong Maltese accent on the other end of the line said, 'Hello, Gordon. My name is Marco. *I'm your father.*'

Hearing my father's voice for the first time in thirty years left me numb. This was almost surreal. We spoke for a while, then made arrangements to meet up a few days later.

My natural father had served fourteen years in prison, for a variety of offences. Now he was living in a small flat down in Mile End, close to the tube station. Flo had bumped into him in Whitechapel High Street. 'I've met our son, Marco,' she told him proudly, and gave him my phone number. I'd rather she hadn't. I'd wanted to wait and contact him in my own good time. But by Flo's account, Marco had been reduced to tears of surprise and joy.

My father and I arranged to meet at his local tube station. I hopped off the Central Line train, looked around and there he was, about five foot six, of stocky build. Short and broad—so that's where I get my physique from. Apart from his shoes and socks, he was wearing just a string vest and trousers. Through the holes in his vest I could see a mass of tattoos and hair.

We went down to the pub and had a drink, while Marco gave me his own version of the break-up with my mother. With pride in his voice, he explained how he had worked for a protection racket, and about his association with the Kray twins in the sixties. Every old villain in London claims to have had dealings with the Kray twins, so whether my father had ever really met them is open to conjecture, but some quality in his voice told me that this story was true. To the criminal fraternity they were both 'diamond geezers', but my natural father's confession seemed to show a tinge of regret.

To give himself some Dutch courage before coming to meet me, he had sniffed some amphetamines—some 'Sulph'. He couldn't look me in the eye as he explained he had taken the drug, and his heavy accent seemed to grow thicker as he hung his head for a few moments.

He explained that he had been married only once, and was now divorced. The marriage had produced six children who were now in their twenties; but there had of course been plenty of other women in his life. So suddenly I now had at least *twelve* brothers and sisters in all; this was all getting too much for me.

When I asked him about his own parents and siblings—my long-lost grandparents, aunts and uncles—he explained that his mum was still alive and living in Australia with the rest of his family. They had emigrated from Malta in the 1950s, but he had chosen not to join them. Marco was downcast that his brothers had done well for themselves while he was the black sheep of the family. How could he visit his family in Sydney, with so little to show for his own life? I tried to persuade him to use the £2,000 he said he had recently received in redundancy money from the local council to visit his mother before she died. He agreed that it would be a sensible move, but I doubted that he would ever see his family again.

(Some days later, I recalled a chance meeting years earlier in a Calcutta dormitory, with an Australian chap of Maltese descent whose surname—I now realised—was the same as that of my own natural father! Sadly, the address book in which I had noted his address was soon lost, when the bag which had contained it was stolen on route from Calcutta to Bangkok. Was this a long-lost cousin?)

I tried to reassure Marco that material gain is less important than a person's self-worth. Spoken while trying to chart my way through a swirling haze of emotion, perhaps my words of comfort only helped to put the lid on any prospect of a trip to Australia. What had this stranger, who was my own father, to feel self-assured about? A broken marriage, protection rackets and a string of convictions? I formed a picture of a very sad man who hadn't really grown up from his teenage years; a comic-book gangster, stalking the rainy streets of Whitechapel. But, at the end of the day, he had been honest with me. I thanked him for that.

We went back to his bed-sit, in the drizzle, and cooked a chicken meal. He gave me a present—a sweat shirt. We talked and ate, as I tried to understand something of this man who had sired me, and then discarded me. Would a small child have been an encumbrance to his 'hard man' image? Would he have wanted me to be like him? I had certainly shared his tastes for women and drugs, the craving for cheap thrills, until my encounter with the risen Christ had rescued me from the pitiful round of self-gratification. Like father, like son? I pondered on what might have been.

On a shelf, I saw a photograph of a family get together apparently some time in the 1960s, and noticed a child of seven or eight, who looked the spitting image of me at that age. It was very disconcerting.

My second meeting with Marco was awful. I turned up at his dingy bed-sit unexpectedly. A woman answered the door, slim with brown hair, ashen faced.

'Is Marco in?' I asked.

'Ah, it's you Gordon,' he shouted from the bedroom, and I went through to see him. He was lying in bed with a broken leg, plaster cast up to his waist, having fallen off a chair while decorating. The anaemic-looking woman went out to the newly-painted bathroom, where I could hear her being sick.

'Where's Tina?' he grumbled. 'Why doesn't she come to see me? Why can't she face me?' Tina, of course, was his eldest child, my full sister. Tina had met neither Marco nor Flo at that time; she was finding it difficult to come to terms with this new family of which she suddenly found herself an unexpected part.

We talked on. The woman went out to be sick for a second time. Marco explained that she was a drug addict experiencing withdrawal. She had been his lover, and had carried his baby—the latest in a long line. The social services were keeping the baby boy in hospital and putting him up for adoption. It was not Marco's choice to reject the baby, but the facts were that my new half-brother was now separated from his mother and father, and was probably facing a lifetime of coming to terms with rejection. The woman, who was an absolute mess, had been a heroin addict until well into the pregnancy and the child had probably been born with a serious heroin addiction.

'All women are weak,' said Marco, as his lover—twenty years his junior—heaved into the toilet basin. I wanted to shout at him; to show him what he was doing. But I didn't want to make a scene with the woman there. It would not have been right to bring her into this; I respected her feelings, even if Marco didn't.

'You pathetic creature,' I thought as I watched him lying bloated in bed. 'What have you done with your life?'

Yet it could have been me lying there, in thirty years' time, a pitiable, burnt-out ruin of a once zestful person. It could easily have been Gordon Barley slouched against the pillow, expecting the world to revolve around him. I was so grateful to God for lifting me off the road to hell, and bringing me into his glorious kingdom.

Marco asked me about my faith and I shared the gospel with him, backing it up with my experiences, as the woman headed for the bathroom for the third time. I was still in a daze at the thought of Marco's baby in hospital waiting for adoption; an echo of myself, thirty years before.

I finally left with my mind swirling in pain and confusion. I had an almost overwhelming desire to get drunk, but somehow I didn't. God was certainly with me that night.

I have never seen my natural father again.

Marco had shown me photographs of himself in his youth, when he had been a good-looking man, and I believed him when he said that women used to fall at his feet. It struck a powerful chord within me. I might not have gone out with a sawn-off shotgun as part of a protection racket, or been involved in vice. Maybe I hadn't exploited women that much, but I'd certainly made a good start along those lines, using my charm to lure them into my bed. Had my lust been caused by something in my jeans, or something in my genes? There, but for Christ, went I.

I am so glad I have been given the opportunity to offer something constructive to humanity through my work at the Mayflower, helping the powerless people of Canning Town to maintain their dignity, and to smooth their ride through East End life.

Now that I have got to know all my new-found siblings, I love each one dearly. They are all easy-going, ordinary folk. And I'm now coming to terms with my emotions. My natural father is not the sort of person I would choose as a friend, someone I would want to be with of my own volition, and I've found it harder to cope with him than my mother. She at least has grown up, even if my father hasn't.

It's funny, but I still find it very difficult to call her Mum, and it was 1994 before I was emotionally capable of sending her a Mother's Day card. Before, it always seemed a betrayal of the woman who brought me up, showing me true maternal love and affection after I had been rejected. As far as I'm concerned, my mother died in 1975.

I don't feel any anger towards Flo. I have forgiven her for her rejection of me. She is full of life and exuberance, but she is quite a sad character too—who wouldn't be after a life like hers? She's a bit of a 'wild card', used to having to shout to be heard, but I've grown to love her. It might seem a small matter for me to start calling her my mum, but my feelings are important, too. Perhaps in time I will, but not just yet.

I still haven't bothered to discover my original Christian name—and, frankly, I don't really care!

I'm Gordon Barley now, and I know who I am.

13

The Living and the Dead

I was content and fulfilled with my role as a community worker, and with my lovely wife, but I had occasionally wondered what else God might have in store for me. As the years went past, I began to think about the ordained ministry, and whether it might be God's will for me to become a parish priest.

Such a job would certainly make use of all the skills I had developed since I had been at the Mayflower, but it would also open up to me a whole range of other exciting and challenging possibilities. Praying for confirmation of this direction, I felt it right to start the ball rolling.

First, I spoke with Edward Furness, whose immediate response was to phone up the Church Pastoral Aid Society (CPAS) and ask them to send me some information. Next stop was a weekend away to find out more about the work of a vicar. That only strengthened my sense of calling.

I had three meetings with the local Director of Ordinands, Robert Howarth, twice on my own and once with Sue present. He suggested that I might want to consider a career with the Church Army, but, after exploring this avenue, I didn't feel that it was the right choice for me. I also spoke with a London City Missioner, and a Free

Church minister, but neither of those roles felt right for me. I felt definitely called to the Anglican priesthood.

I was referred to David Lowman, the Diocesan Director of Ordinands, and former ABM selector and secretary. ABM stands for Advisory Board for Ministry; it is the body that interviews and 'screens' potential ordinands, reporting to the candidate's bishop, who takes the final decision whether to send someone forward for training.

David Lowman soon set me to work reading books and writing reviews about them in my spare time; I wrote essays for him to establish whether I had the academic ability to complete the rigorous course of training, if I were to be approved by a selection conference—and also to gain a greater understanding of the role of the priesthood. I spoke with another Anglican clergyman, and began attending St John's Church, Stratford, just up the road from the Mayflower, in order to learn more of how an Anglican parish operates.

It was clearly going to be a long haul, but I had expected that, and I was ready for it. My work at the Mayflower and my hospital chaplaincy work went on. And I continued to spend time counselling for Reachout Trust. I prayed that God's will for my future might be clearly seen by those responsible for ensuring that the right people are trained to become the crucial next generation of vicars.

While this series of meetings was progressing, my sister's mental health took another turn for the worse towards the end of 1992. Her relationship with her husband had been floundering for some time; it sometimes crossed my mind that Doug had only married Sharon for the cash my dad had left her, along with the money she got from me for her share of the family house. Though they had a second child together, a year or two after Dad's death, the stormy marriage was soon on the rocks.

There had been some family upset when Doug's sister

verbally attacked Sharon, triggering a row which resulted in Doug's brother kicking a door down and other family members calling Sharon names in the street.

Poor Sharon seemed always to be just going into hospital or just coming out. There were allegations that she and another woman had gone off with two other blokes, and a whole parcel of other mischievous mud slinging. First the couple were going to split up, then they resolved to try to make one last try to make a success of their marriage. In a pathetic attempt to save their relationship, the crazy pair decided to have yet another baby.

I tried in vain to talk Sharon out of this. While she was in hospital for her fourth confinement, her husband began an affair with a woman who lived around the corner. Sharon came home, saw what was happening, and was unable to cope. She had a serious nervous breakdown. She was found screaming her head off at the kids, and the neighbours called the police and she was taken away.

The new baby is now being brought up by a cousin, who has a custody order but is desperate to adopt, while the other two children are with their father—who is now associating with a woman with three children of her own.

Sharon was committed to Warley psychiatric hospital, Brentwood, where she seemed to revert back to childhood. Incapable of caring for herself, she needed to be washed and bathed by nurses. She was even afraid to go to the toilet on her own. I couldn't begin to understand the depths of depression that she has suffered. Many might want to condemn her life and actions, but I'm absolutely certain that God doesn't condemn her, and neither do I. She is, and will always be, my sister and I love her dearly.

She still pines for her middle two children, whom she had been bringing up herself, though she seems to have no strong maternal affection for her final baby from whom she was separated a few weeks after birth.

Eighteen months later, she was fantasising about coming to live with Sue and me, but I have made it clear that such a course of action is out of the question. She has such deep needs, as an adult person acting like a child, that we couldn't possibly cope, and the strain would probably destroy our own marriage.

People who are mentally ill are often extremely self-centred. The whole world has to revolve around them, and only full-time professional people have the time, the resources and the training to provide adequate care. Neighbours, relatives and friends cannot provide anything like the necessary attention.

I visit her as regularly as I am able. It can be an alarming experience to visit a psychiatric ward for the first time, and to see women walking around with mis-matched clothing, make-up they've put on anyhow, and an unkempt shock of white hair sticking up on end. Conversations are disjointed and child-like, often about everyday incidents that are wildly distorted or completely fabricated. Many have crazed expressions, or are unable to express themselves at all. Some walk about with contorted limbs, or—in the case of paranoid schizophrenia—are convinced that they are being persecuted. But they are all God's children.

As I was sitting with Sharon once, an elderly lady—perhaps excited by watching the chunky lifeguards in *Baywatch*, which was on the ward television set—came up and wanted to kiss me. I offered my cheek to this senile lady, almost bald and with no teeth. She planted a big wet smacker on my cheek and went away contented. No worries! She's someone's daughter, someone's sister, someone's wife. She's not a freak, she's a person deserving of dignity, understanding and compassion. Visiting a psychiatric ward no longer held any anxieties for me. My heart goes out to all those who have lost their slender hold on reality, and whose grasp on their own sanity has slipped away under the pressure of everyday living. It could have happened to me.

For Christmas 1992 Sue and I went up to stay with her parents, in the Yorkshire coastal town of Filey. I really enjoyed being with Sue's dad. He was blunt and direct, and you always knew just where you stood with him. He and I used to go out regularly for a pint together. I would tell him about my world travels, and he would regale me with anecdotes of his time in the Army Educational Corp.

He was always sending off short stories for competitions, and one of his keenest desires was to get a book published. (This book's for you, Dad. I hope you like it!)

On our last trip down to the pub that Christmas, I got to the end of my story and explained how I had come to be a follower of Christ. I shared the gospel with him, explaining how Christ had died in order that we might have abundant life in peace and fellowship with our creator. There was a moment of silence, then we put on our coats to head home.

It was a starry night as we walked back. He went out into the garden for a smoke—he didn't smoke in the house, from respect for other people—and he pointed out the various constellations to me. 'There's Orion, lad.'

As we finally sat down in the kitchen, I told him how much I appreciated having him as my father-in-law.

'It's more than that though, isn't it?' he said.

'Yes, it's much more than that,' I replied, my eyes a little moist. We were like father and son. It felt like home here. It was so long since I'd had a real father.

When he dropped us off at the station next morning, Sue commented that her dad didn't look well. About a week later, the telephone rang one evening. Sue picked it up, and I watched as her face turned ashen. It was Sue's mother calling. She'd just found her husband lying motionless on the bed. Fearing the worst, she had immediately called the doctor, but it was too late. There would be no more long talks for Sue's dad and me. I turned to comfort my distraught wife.

Next day, we went back up to Filey to be with Sue's mum. She was coping wonderfully well. By the time we arrived, with sympathetic neighbours rallying around, she had made all the funeral arrangements.

'He really thought a lot of you, and he wasn't the sort of person to do that with many people,' Sue's mother told me. 'He picked and chose who he would be friends with.'

A friend of mine also experienced the tragic loss of his father, only a week after Sue and I were bereaved, and just two months after losing his mother. 'You can't negotiate with death,' he reflected. 'It's like a spectral bailiff who comes uninvited into your life, seizes your loved one and carries him off without a by-your-leave.'

It was with a heavy heart from this sudden loss of my third 'father' that I continued my occasional meetings with David Lowman, to establish whether I was ever even going to be sent to a selection conference. From the essays I'd written it was clear that I had the potential to complete the training course, but my academic ability needed to be brought up to a satisfactory standard. There is a home study project called the Aston Training Scheme, which the Anglican church uses to bring candidates of low academic achievement up to scratch before sending them to theological college. It's also used to stretch and challenge academics by giving them some life experience. This was potentially a way forward for me; but I had first to convince my bishop that I was suitable material for the priesthood.

David Lowman sent me to see Canon Thompson, the vice-provost of Chelmsford Cathedral, for a second opinion. We got on well, talking for an hour or more, and the Canon reported back favourably about me to David Lowman. I was finally put forward to be vetted by the Bishop of

Barking, former Mayflower Warden Roger Sainsbury, who heartily agreed to send me to selection conference.

Early in 1994, I travelled down the East India Dock Road to an ABM conference in Limehouse. I'd just passed my driving test the month before, so I was in an optimistic mood. The four selectors were lovely people to whom I warmed very easily, and the tough three-day conference went without hitch. Along with the fifteen or so other candidates, I was put through my paces, with various written tests, discussion groups and private interviews. I felt strongly upheld by prayer from the Mayflower, St John's, the chaplaincy team, Pilgrim's Hall and dozens of individual Christians.

I came away knowing that I had given my very best, and there was no way in which I could have done better. I went straight off afterwards to another conference in connection with my work at the Mayflower, then Sue and I went away together for a week's break at Lee Abbey, a holiday and conference centre.

The writer Adrian Plass was the guest speaker that week, and he happened to sit next to me at breakfast one morning. When I mentioned to him that I was working on this book, he said, 'Having someone put together a book about your life is rather like undergoing a prolonged period of psychotherapy.' Never were truer words spoken!

Sue and I returned home refreshed from Lee Abbey, to find an envelope awaiting me on the doormat. It was the results of the selection conference. My heart was pounding as I opened it. With the proviso that I first spend two years on the Aston Training Scheme, I had been accepted to train towards ordination! David Lowman and Bishop Roger both tendered their warmest congratulations. I was ecstatic!

If all goes according to plan, I will continue at the Mayflower through till mid-1996, studying in the evenings and at weekends. They have generously given me two days off each week to further my studies; and they continue to pay me for one of those days. Then I go to theological college for two years before I get ordained and begin my first curacy in 1998. As I write this, I should be a priest by the end of the century, and become a portly vicar sometime early in the next millennium! It all seems a very long way off. . . .

Sue and I are excited about the prospect of working together. A vicar and his wife can be a unique working team which could evolve into a joint ministry. Sue has a heart for refugees, and a gift for counselling, so . . . who knows?

I'm grateful for the opportunity I was given to come and work in Canning Town back in 1989 when I feared that I might be completely unemployable. I've been trained and nurtured, allowed to use my own initiative, and really to come out and grow—to find the real 'me'. I've had a lot of rough edges knocked off me as I've struggled to sort myself out, and to grow in God. It has been exciting to work out my faith in a vibrant Christian centre and a place of vision.

With my sights on the future, I want to be where the action is—and that probably means a pioneering church development in the inner city, where my Mayflower experiences can come in useful. But I want to be flexible. Some people might think that, with my particular background, I should be working with New Age travellers and other nonconformist types, but I don't want to be stereotyped.

Now that I have found Christ; met and married my partner for life; become reunited with my natural family; found a role in life, as a friend to the poor and powerless; learned to help those who are deceived by the cults, as I once was myself; and discovered a whole new career opening up in the Anglican Church; I feel that at last I have almost arrived safely 'home'.

No great unfulfilled ambitions remain, except perhaps to go trekking around South America with Sue for a few weeks, if I can find a suitable gap in my training. (Oh, and I'd like to be a rock'n'roll singer, too!) There are still obstacles in my path, but I know God is with me. He brought me out of my dark depression and despair into the eternal glow of his glorious light.

Looking back, there have been in my life both problems of my own making and other people's problems that have adversely affected me. The parental rejection, the alienation I felt from bereavement, my sister's fragile mental health, many of the crises during my travelling days, and the trials of being a community worker in the inner city, all affected me.

I certainly created my fair share of misery for myself. It may be a popular male fantasy to have dozens of women falling at your feet, but my promiscuous lifestyle spoiled my ability to form meaningful relationships for a long time. My occasional dishonesty and petty crime were purely for my own gain. And travelling was pure self-indulgence most of the time.

Nobody forced drugs down my throat, or pushed joints into my hand; I took them of my own free will, and they severely distorted my concept of reality. I drank too much, but unlike many alcoholics who have to kick the habit completely before it destroys them, I have managed to turn myself into an occasional, social drinker.

My experiences with cults and world religions were all part of an exotic spiritual quest—though I didn't realise that I was on one at the time. After seven months in the 'Moonies', weeks spent on Indian ashrams, dabbling in mysticism and New Age philosophies, an interest in paganism and primitive religions, long periods of meditation in a Buddhist monastery, first-hand encounters with Judaism, and experience of Islam, it's strange to think that I should eventually find spiritual fulfilment in a fresh understanding of the richness and authenticity of my childhood faith—and that my decision to follow Christ should be made a couple of miles down the road from the house where I grew up!

Now I'm on the right path, at last, and I'm going to keep going on down that narrow road, following in Christ's footsteps. After an inauspicious beginning—and a traumatic middle!—life is working out for me now. I pray that the countless others who are experiencing problems and worries or who are broken on the wheel of misfortune and despair, will also find the peace of mind that comes from knowing the risen Christ.

God generously gave me many opportunities to come to know his love. I could have persisted in the commitment I made at a crusade during my teens; I could have heeded the Levicks in my youth; I could have listened to the followers of Christ whom I met in Israel, on the boat to Greece, in India, or Australia. Then there was an opportunity in Spain. I could have walked into most churches in Britain and been warmly received. Instead, I took a long and strange road home to God.

I didn't take up any of those heaven-sent opportunities, but God kept reaching out to me and calling my name, until eventually I turned and ran into the open arms of a Father who will never reject or leave me—to be enveloped in his glorylove.

How many further opportunities might he graciously have given for me to come to him? The number would not have been limitless. Eventually death comes to us all, in a strange and unexpected hour, unplanned for, like a thief on a moonless night. We are all finite people craving the infinite, for only in the deathless love of a resurrected God can we truly find ourselves.

If you are as I was—a slave to drink, drugs, sex, travel,

mysticism, hedonism, pure self-indulgence in all its forms—then I know exactly where that road you travel is going to lead you in the end. When the next joint or drink doesn't taste so good, when you're having sexual intercourse with someone whose name you forgot to ask, when you're tearing your hair out in despair, sobbing in your lonely bed, or being swept along in the mad rush of material excess; when the darkness seems to be closing in around you—as it closed in on me—just remember that the only person in the vast universe who can truly help you is just a prayer away.

Now is the time to turn towards home. Who knows? It may be your last chance.